THE WORLD
OF THE
BRONTËS

For Shirley

"no coward soul"

Design copyright © 1997 Carlton Books Limited
Text copyright © 1997 Jane O'Neill

First published in Canada in 1997 by Raincoast Books
8680 Cambie Street
Vancouver, B.C.
V6P 6M9
(604) 323–7100

Canadian Cataloguing in Publication Data
O'Neill, Jane
The world of the Brontës

Includes index
ISBN 1-55192-121-9

1. Brontë, Charlotte. 1816-1855–Biography. 2. Brontë, Emily. 1818-
1848–Biography. 3. Brontë, Anne, 1820-1849–Biography. 4. Authors, English,
19th Century–Biography. I.Title
PR4168.O56 1997   823'.809   C97–910461-0

Project Editor: Sarah Larter
Art Direction: Zoë Maggs
Designer: Simon Mercer
Picture Research: Lorna Ainger
Production: Sarah Schuman

Printed and bound in Italy

THE WORLD
OF THE
BRONTËS

The lives, times and works of

Charlotte, Emily and Anne Brontë

Jane O'Neill

RAINCOAST BOOKS

Vancouver

CONTENTS

ABOVE: ANNE BRONTË "WHAT YOU
PLEASE", JULY 25, 1840.
LEFT: BRONTË FALLS, NEAR
HAWORTH.

INTRODUCTION

EVEN IN THE BRONTËS' LIFETIME, interest in their lives and interest in their novels were intertwined. No sooner was *Jane Eyre* published and a success, than a rumour started doing the rounds that it was the work of the governess of Thackeray's daughters. More accurate rumours succeeded that one, and with the publication of *Shirley*, with identifiable places and people, the identity of the author became common knowledge in Yorkshire and the North generally.

With that knowledge came the first tourists. "Various folks are beginning to come to Haworth, on the wise errand of seeing the scenery described in *Jane Eyre* and *Shirley*", wrote Charlotte unenthusiastically. When, after her death, Mrs Gaskell wrote the classic *Life*, she ensured that our reading of the novels and poems was influenced by the sisters' fellow novelist's views of their lives, works and fates. Even today there are many members of the Brontë Society who are lukewarm about the novels but avidly interested in the minutiæ of their lives. With some novelists the works are all, and speculation about their lives is at best secondary: Fielding, Trollope, Henry James are such writers. With the Brontës one interest feeds the other.

Over the century and a half since their deaths, the Brontës have assumed various guises in the popular imagination. For Mrs Gaskell Charlotte was close to a saint: a martyr to duty who uncomplainingly bore a variety of crosses, including a half-mad father, seclusion in a brutal and uncultivated village, and even an uncongenial sister: all she could learn about Emily, Mrs Gaskell said, had not tended to give her a "pleasant impression of her" – surely the most perverse and inadequate summary of Emily's character ever made. With time all of Charlotte's crosses have been shown to be exaggerations or misinterpretations, and new images of Charlotte and her sisters have taken the place of that brilliantly conveyed first, gloomy picture. Emily has been a lonely, mystic visionary, a lesbian, even a sufferer from anorexia – she the cook of the family! Anne has changed from the "gentle Anne" of Ellen Nussey's account to a campaigner for women's rights, a believer in universal salvation, an ironist in the Jane Austen mould. Charlotte has borne the main feminist interest, has received many a drubbing for conveying an image of her sisters that the drubber dislikes, and, in Juliet Barker's recent and magisterial biography of the whole family, emerges as a rather unlikeable, self-pitying, viragoish creature.

To go to the parsonage at Haworth is to get perhaps the most complete picture of the close, gifted family, feeding off each other's creativity: the little books and the tiny pictures, the samplers worked under Aunt Branwell's eyes, Branwell's perfunctory oil paintings. Here we can appreciate the closeness with the servants, the more distant relations with the rest of Haworth, the stimulus of having a remarkable man as a father who was also a published writer. All are there: the beginnings, the stimuli, the excursions to the outside world, the finished works of genius. And the next best thing to coming to the museum is a work such as Jane O'Neill's, one that marries words and pictures to give as complete an impression as we can get of these remarkable lives.

DR ROBERT BARNARD
CHAIRMAN, THE BRONTË SOCIETY

THE PARSONAGE AT HAWORTH.

CHRONOLOGY

1777

MARCH 17: Patrick Brontë born in Emdale, County Down, Ireland on St Patrick's day.

1783

APRIL 15: Maria Branwell born in Penzance, Cornwall.

1802

OCTOBER 1: Patrick Brontë enters St John's College Cambridge, where he studies Theology and Classics.

1806

Patrick Brontë takes Holy Orders, in the Church of England. His first curacy is at Wethersfield in Essex, where he remains for three years.

1809

Patrick is appointed curate at All Saints' Church, Wellington in Shropshire.

1809–11

Patrick in Yorkshire where he is curate in Dewsbury for two years, before becoming minister at Hartshead Church.

1812

Patrick meets Maria Branwell; they marry on December 29.

1814

JANUARY: Maria Brontë born (exact date unknown), baptised at Hartshead Church, April 23.

1815

FEBRUARY 8: Elizabeth Brontë born, baptised Thornton Church, August 26.
Patrick becomes Perpetual Curate of Thornton Church.

1816

APRIL 21: Charlotte Brontë born, baptised at Thornton Church, June 29.

1817

JUNE 26: Patrick Branwell Brontë, the only son of Maria and Patrick, born, baptised at Thornton, July 23.

1818

JULY 30: Emily Jane Brontë born, baptised at Thornton, August 20.

1820

JANUARY 17: Anne Brontë born, baptised at Thornton, March 25.
FEBRUARY: Patrick appointed Perpetual Curate of Haworth. It is to be the Brontë home for the rest of their lives.

1821

MAY: Elizabeth Branwell comes to the Parsonage to nurse her terminally ill sister and take charge of the household.
SEPTEMBER 15: Mrs Maria Brontë dies of cancer and is buried at Haworth Church.

1824

JULY: Maria and Elizabeth arrive at the Clergy Daughters' School at Cowan Bridge, Charlotte follows in August and Emily in November.

1825

FEBRUARY 14: Maria, very ill, leaves Cowan Bridge. She dies at Haworth on May 6.
MAY 31: Elizabeth, also very ill, leaves Cowan Bridge. The next day Patrick withdraws Charlotte and Emily from the school.
JUNE 15: Elizabeth dies at Haworth.

1831

JANUARY: Charlotte is sent to Miss Wooler's school at Roe Head, Mirfield, near Huddersfield. Here she meets her two close, lifelong friends, Ellen Nussey and Mary Taylor. She returns to Haworth the next year to teach her sisters.

1835

Charlotte returns to Roe Head, this time as a teacher, taking Emily with her as a pupil. Emily, suffering from extreme homesickness, returns to Haworth after six months.

1836

JANUARY: Anne goes to Roe Head in Emily's place.

1837

DECEMBER: Anne leaves Roe Head, which has moved to Dewsbury Moor.

1838

SEPTEMBER: Emily goes to teach at Miss Patchett's school at Law Hill, Halifax; she stays just six months.

DECEMBER: Charlotte leaves Miss Wooler's school.

1839

APRIL: Anne becomes governess to the Ingham family, Mirfield; she leaves the post in December.

MAY: Charlotte goes as governess to the Sidgwick family, near Skipton; she leaves the position after just two months.

1840

JANUARY: Branwell becomes tutor to the Postlethwaite family at Broughton in Furness; he is dismissed after just six months.

MAY: Anne goes as governess to the Robinson family at Thorp Green Hall, near York.

AUGUST: Branwell becomes a clerk on the Leeds–Manchester railway.

1841

MARCH: Charlotte goes as governess to the White family at Rawdon; she leaves the post in December of the same year.

1842

FEBRUARY: Charlotte and Emily travel to Brussels to study at the Pensionnat Heger.

MARCH: Branwell is dismissed from his position as clerk-in-charge at Luddenden Foot railway station.

OCTOBER 29: Aunt Branwell dies and is buried at Haworth.

NOVEMBER: Charlotte and Emily return from Brussels.

1843

JANUARY: Branwell accompanies Anne to Thorp Green to act as tutor to Edmund Robinson. Charlotte returns to Brussels without Emily.

1844

JANUARY: Charlotte returns to Haworth from Brussels, hopelessly in love with M. Heger.

1845

JUNE: Anne leaves Thorp Green permanently.

JULY: Branwell is dismissed from Thorp Green, after becoming involved with the mistress of the house, Lydia Robinson. Charlotte "discovers" Emily's poems and suggests a joint publication with her own and Anne's poems.

1846

MAY: Poems by Currer, Ellis and Acton Bell (Charlotte, Emily and Anne Brontë) is published at the sisters' own expense. The book attracts little notice and only two copies are sold.

JUNE: Charlotte finishes *The Professor*, but fails to find a publisher. Emily completes *Wuthering Heights* and Anne *Agnes Grey*.

AUGUST: Charlotte and her father go to Manchester, where he has an operation for cataracts; here she begins to write *Jane Eyre*.

1847

OCTOBER: *Jane Eyre* is published by Smith, Elder – it is instantly hailed a masterpiece.

DECEMBER: *Agnes Grey* and *Wuthering Heights* published by Thomas Cautley Newby. *Agnes Grey* attracts little attention; critics are shocked by *Wuthering Heights*.

1848

JUNE: *The Tenant of Wildfell Hall* published.

JULY: Charlotte and Anne travel to London to reveal their identities to their publishers and the public; Emily refuses to go.

SEPTEMBER 24: Branwell dies of tuberculosis and is buried at Haworth Church.

DECEMBER 19: Emily dies of tuberculosis and is buried in Haworth Church.

1849

MAY 28: Anne dies of tuberculosis in Scarborough, where she is buried.

OCTOBER: *Shirley,* Charlotte's second published novel, is published by Smith, Elder.

NOVEMBER–DECEMBER: Charlotte visits London where she stays with her publisher, George Smith; while there, she meets the writers Harriet Martineau and William Makepeace Thackeray.

1850

Charlotte meets Mrs Gaskell, who becomes a good friend. A memorial edition of *Wuthering Heights* and *Agnes Grey* is published complete with "A Biographical notice of Ellis and Acton Bell" and unpublished poems and manuscripts by Anne and Emily.

1853

JANUARY: *Villette* is published.

1854

APRIL: Arthur Bell Nicholls' proposal is accepted by Charlotte.

JUNE: Charlotte marries Arthur Bell Nicholls, despite her father's reservations. They honeymoon in Ireland.

1855

MARCH 31: Charlotte dies in the early stages of pregnancy.

1857

MARCH: Mrs Gaskell's *Life of Charlotte Brontë*, written with the blessing of Patrick Brontë, is published by Smith, Elder. In June they publish *The Professor*, Charlotte's first novel.

1861

JUNE 7: Patrick Brontë dies, aged 84.

1906

DECEMBER 2: Arthur Bell Nicholls dies, aged 88, in Ireland.

1 WHO WERE THE BRONTËS?

IN THE AUTUMN OF 1847 *Jane Eyre* was first published, followed less than two months later by *Agnes Grey* and *Wuthering Heights*. The three novels were published under the now famous pseudonyms of Currer, Acton and Ellis Bell. Who were these people? This question set alight the whole literary world of the day.

The publisher of *Jane Eyre* records his response to the manuscript. "After breakfast I took the MS. of 'Jane Eyre' to my little study, and began to read it. The story quickly took me captive … I could not put the book down … before I went to bed that night I had finished reading the manuscript." He was not alone in his admiration, and when *Wuthering Heights* and *Agnes Grey* appeared that December, curiosity was fuelled about the real identity of these writers.

It was not until July 1848 – amid mounting speculation that Currer Bell had written all three novels – that Charlotte (Currer Bell) and Anne (Acton Bell) decided to go to their London publisher and reveal their identities as three separate sisters – Charlotte, Emily and Anne Brontë. Emily (Ellis Bell) refused to accompany them and was, indeed, very angry that her identity was included in the revelations.

Charlotte, the eldest of the three, was thirty-one years old in 1847, Emily twenty-nine, and Anne twenty-seven. They had lived since 1820 in the small, hilly Yorkshire town of Haworth, where their Irish father, Patrick, was Perpetual Curate of the parish church. The Parsonage at the top of the hill had become their much-loved home. It had shared in the kind of tragic loss

common in Haworth in the 1820s: within eighteen months of their arrival, Patrick was left a widower and his six children motherless; in 1825 the two oldest, Maria and Elizabeth, died of tuberculosis.

What their artistic contribution might have been will never be known. What their deaths meant, however, was that Charlotte and Emily were brought back from the boarding school where their older siblings had become ill to be educated at the Parsonage. The four remaining children – Charlotte, Branwell, Emily and Anne – were thus free to indulge together their outstanding imaginations. As soon as they could write – and no doubt even before – they were making up stories and creating characters; in the juvenilia the seeds of the novelists were already germinating.

Although he never fulfilled his early promise, Branwell – the only boy in the family – played a very important part in the development of his sisters' genius. That his own life was ruined by excessive use of drugs and alcohol was a tragedy for them all.

What his sisters achieved is especially remarkable because they were not allowed long to achieve it. Anne and Emily died at the ages of twenty-nine and thirty respectively, while Charlotte, who outlived all her siblings, lived until thirty-nine. Her desolate grief at the loss of those with whom she had shared all her creative and imaginative life echoes down the years:

One by one I have watched them fall asleep on my arm –
I have seen them buried one by one …

THE PORTRAIT OF THE BRONTË SISTERS PAINTED BY THEIR BROTHER BRANWELL, C.1834. KNOWN AS "THE PILLAR PORTRAIT", IT LAY FOLDED IN A CUPBOARD FOR MANY YEARS. FROM THE LEFT: ANNE, EMILY AND CHARLOTTE; THE SPACE BETWEEN EMILY AND CHARLOTTE IS WHERE THERE WAS ONCE A PORTRAIT OF BRANWELL.

PATRICK

PHOTOGRAPH OF PATRICK, TAKEN IN THE FINAL YEARS OF HIS LIFE.

BORN ON ST PATRICK'S DAY 1777, Patrick Brontë's life was to span the Romantic period and the first twenty-four years of Victorian England. He outlived not only his wife but all his six children, dying at the age of eighty-four in 1861. The story of his life, from very modest beginnings to Perpetual Curate of Haworth and father of three famous children, is a remarkable one. Elizabeth Gaskell, Charlotte's contemporary and her first biographer describes his background:

The Rev. Patrick Brontë is a native of the county Down in Ireland. His father, Hugh Brontë, was left an orphan at an early age. He came from the south to the north of the island, and settled in the parish of Ahaderg, near Loughbrickland. There was some family tradition that, humble as Hugh Brontë's circumstances were, he was the descendant of an ancient family. But about this he nor his descendants have cared to inquire. He made an early marriage, and reared and educated ten children on the proceeds of the few acres of land which he farmed. This large family were remarkable for great physical strength, and much personal beauty. Even in his old age, Mr Brontë is a striking-looking man, above the common height, with a nobly shaped head, and erect carriage. In his youth he must have been unusually handsome.

She goes on to say that his father could give him no financial help and at the age of sixteen, ambitious to do well, he "opened a public school", later becoming tutor to the children of the Reverend Mr Tighe before proceeding to St John's College, Cambridge.

GRAND DESIGNS

Patrick was born in a two-roomed traditional Irish cabin in Emdale, Drumballyroney. Although his origins were "humble", the family were never as poor as the image of the cabin suggests. Nevertheless, for an Irishman of his class and background to proceed to Cambridge was most unusual. As Juliet Barker has pointed out, it was made possible by several happy circumstances. Patrick was employed as tutor to the sons of the Reverend

Thomas Tighe, who was himself a graduate of St John's College, Cambridge and could vouch for Patrick's ability and suitability. St John's had more funds available for helping impoverished intelligent students than any other college or university of the time; it also had strong Evangelical Christian connections, which made it sympathetic to a young man of Patrick's religious persuasions. In addition, Patrick was sponsored by an eminent Evangelical, Henry Thornton, and by Thornton's cousin, William Wilberforce. It must have been clear, at this early stage in Patrick's life, that he was a young man worth educating for a career in the Church.

It was on entering Cambridge that Patrick assumed for the first time the name of Bronte. In Ireland the family was known by various versions of the name: Prunty, Brunty and Bruntee, possibly others. For Patrick, embarking on what he hoped would be a distinguished career, it must have been an important moment to be matched by an important and significant name: only a year before Lord Nelson, one of Patrick's heroes, had assumed the title of the Duke of Bronte. To Patrick, the change in the spelling of his name must have appeared both wholly justifiable – a mere standardizing – as well as symbolic of the new, and important, direction his life was taking.

It is clear that the tall, thin, red-haired student with the Irish accent was anxious to do well and leave his mark on the world. In addition to his studies, Patrick was able to indulge what was to prove a lifelong interest in things military by joining the local militia. No doubt Branwell – who was himself fascinated by war and its tactics – would later hear all about how Patrick had

been drilled by Lord Palmerston while a student at Cambridge – a fact of which the Reverend Brontë was very proud.

Like his children, Patrick had literary aspirations and, while he was furthering his career in the Church in various curacies, he published several volumes of poetry, the best known of which is probably *Cottage Poems*. In them, his message is clear: lead a good Christian life – however humble – and in the life to come you'll "wear a bright Immortal crown". Patrick's exhortations and moral lessons were not confined to his writing. He lived by the code which he preached, campaigning tirelessly for the causes he believed in.

PATRICK THE FATHER

As a father, Patrick has often been criticized as stern and autocratic, a legacy that has come down to us from Mrs Gaskell's biography of Charlotte, in which she describes him as a distant, rather frightening and selfish character, who needed to be placated and humoured. Juliet Barker paints a different picture. She cites a friend of both Patrick and Branwell, William Dearden, who refutes a number of Mrs Gaskell's criticisms of Mr Brontë. According to Dearden, Branwell had told him that, on his mother's death, "his father watched over his little bereaved flock with truly paternal solicitude and affection … he was their constant guardian and instructor – and … he took a lively interest in all their innocent amusements." In many ways, of course, he was an ideal father for his creative children, encouraging the development of their intellectual and imaginative interests, and allowing them surprisingly liberal access to a wide range of books and leading newspapers and magazines of the day.

In his last years, after the death of Charlotte, Patrick was looked after by Arthur Bell Nicholls, his curate and Charlotte's widower, who remained at the Parsonage until Patrick's death. Although Patrick's literary ambitions were unfulfilled, it was clearly a matter of great pride and satisfaction to him that his children, particularly Charlotte, had succeeded in making the Brontë name known throughout the world.

PORTRAIT OF PATRICK AS A YOUNG MAN.

PATRICK, TOO – LIKE HIS FAMOUS CHILDREN – HAD SOME OF HIS WORK PUBLISHED.

P A T R I C K

MARIA

"**M**Y DEAR SAUCY PAT – Now don't you think you deserve this epithet, far more, than I do that which you have given me?" wrote Maria Branwell to Patrick Brontë on November 18, 1812. All we know of the mother of the Brontë children suggests that she was a lively, intelligent woman who would have delighted in the family she created with her "Saucy Pat".

AN EARLY PORTRAIT OF MARIA BRANWELL.

Maria Branwell came of a well-established and prominent Cornish family. Her father, a successful grocer and tea-merchant in Penzance, provided a stable, comfortable home for his wife and children, and Maria grew up in what was a prominent family in the town at the end of the eighteenth century. That the country was at war with France for much of her youth does not seem to have affected her life in any material way, although she would have been aware of the warships in the Channel and the restrictions on trade which affected local businesses. The family were Wesleyan Methodists, and it was at the Wesleyan School at Woodhouse Grove near Bradford that Patrick and Maria met.

Maria was twenty-nine when she left Cornwall and went to live with her uncle and aunt in Yorkshire. Juliet Barker describes her at this time as, "petite and elegant though not pretty; pious and something of a blue-stocking but also of a bright, cheerful and witty disposition." Both her parents had died and she had been living with two of her sisters in Penzance. When various circumstances resulted in the family splitting up, she made the decision to leave the security of a place where her family was well known and respected to carve out a new life for herself.

A NEW LIFE

Her uncle by marriage, John Fennell, whom Patrick had known in Wellington, was the newly appointed headmaster of Woodhouse Grove, and Maria came to the school both to help her aunt with the domestic running of the establishment and as a companion to her cousin Jane. Jane had recently become engaged to the Reverend William Morgan, Patrick's good friend and fellow curate at All Saints' Church, Wellington. It was, therefore, quite natural that the three men should meet again in Yorkshire and that John Fennell should call on Patrick to provide help at the school.

In July 1812 Patrick was invited to examine the boys of Woodhouse Grove in the Classics, and it was while he was there that he first met Maria. By the end of

CHARLOTTE BRONTË'S
COPY OF A PORTRAIT
OF HER MOTHER,
PAINTED IN 1830
WHEN CHARLOTTE WAS
FOURTEEN YEARS OLD.

occasioned great sorrow of heart to me and was an irreparable loss to both me and my children.

Maria must have found life as a clergyman's wife in the industrial north very different from the one she was used to in Cornwall, although the years the family spent at Thornton seem to have been very happy ones. There she formed a close and important friendship with Elizabeth Firth, the daughter of a local doctor, who welcomed the Brontës into her wide circle of friends. Maria's doubts about her suitability for the life that lay ahead are expressed in one of her "courtship" letters in which she had written, "I feel that my heart is more ready to attach itself to earth than heaven. I sometimes think there never was a mind so dull and inactive as mine is with regard to spiritual things." But her last letter before her marriage suggests that she was a very fitting wife for her clergyman husband. In it she talks of how much she hopes to "improve in every religious and moral quality" so that she can be of a help to Patrick, "edify others" and "bring glory" to God.

At Thornton, despite her frequent pregnancies, Maria still found time to write *The Advantages of Poverty in Religious Concerns*, which is dismissed by Wise and Symington with, "It abounds in the obvious".

AN IRREPARABLE LOSS

Maria Brontë produced six children during her nine years of marriage to Patrick. She died of cancer in 1821, seventeen months after the family moved to Haworth.

When she died, her eldest child, also called Maria, was seven years old; the youngest, Anne, was twenty months. It is not difficult to imagine the mental and emotional anguish she must have suffered – in addition to the prolonged physical pain – at the thought of leaving behind so young and vulnerable a family. The servants bore witness to her distress on their account, and the nurse reported her calling out repeatedly, "Oh God my poor children – oh God my poor children!"

August she had agreed to marry him; and on December 29 they had a joint wedding ceremony with Jane Fennell and William Morgan, each of the bridegrooms conducting the marriage service for the other couple.

Many years later, after the deaths of her siblings, Patrick was to give Charlotte her mother's letters and papers to read. Much moved, she was to say of them:

> *The papers were yellow with time, all having been written before I was born; it was strange now to peruse, for the first time, the records of a mind whence mine own sprang; and most strange, and at once sad and sweet, to find that mind of a truly fine, pure and elevated order. They were written to papa before they were married. There is a rectitude, a refinement, a constancy, a modesty, a sense, a gentleness about them indescribable. I wish she had lived, and that I had known her.*

One wonders, of course now, how different the lives of the Brontë children would have been had their mother lived to bring them up. As Mrs Gaskell reports Patrick saying,

> *In a modest competency my wife and I lived in as much happiness as can be expected in this world – for nine years. At the end of that time, alas! She died, which*

HOMES BEFORE
HAWORTH

HARTSHEAD CHURCH, NEAR CLECKHEATON, KIRKLEES, WEST YORKSHIRE. WHILE CURATE THERE, PATRICK BRONTË MET AND MARRIED MARIA BRANWELL. IT WAS WHILE HE WAS THERE THAT LUDDITE VIOLENCE IN THE AREA WAS AT ITS HEIGHT.

PATRICK, AND THEN THE BRONTË family, made their home in several places, from Essex to Yorkshire before they settled at Haworth – the most famous Brontë residence.

WETHERSFIELD AND WELLINGTON

Having received his degree from Cambridge University, Patrick Brontë went on to be ordained in the Church of England, and by October 1806 he was officiating at services at St Mary Magdalene, the parish church of Wethersfield, a small, attractive Essex village where he had been appointed to his first curacy. The vicar, Joseph Jowett, was Regius Professor of Civil Law at Cambridge, whose duties at the University meant that he was often absent from his parish, leaving Patrick considerable freedom and autonomy.

It was while Patrick was at Wethersfield that he met and fell in love with Mary Burder, the daughter of a well-to-do farmer. The accepted version of what happened to thwart the pair's marriage is that her family, considering Patrick unsuitable as a husband, opposed it. Juliet Barker suggests, however, that it was Patrick himself who withdrew from the intended union, probably because Mary was a Congregationalist and their marriage could have been an impediment in his career in the Church of England. If this interpretation of events is true, it would explain why Mary reacted in such a hostile manner when, lonely after Maria's death and desperate for a replacement mother for his six children, Patrick tried to renew his attentions to her.

In January 1809, Patrick left Wethersfield to take up a new post as assistant curate of All Saints' Church, which was in the town of Wellington in the midlands county of Shropshire.

This was Patrick's first exposure to an industrial town, a far cry from rural Wethersfield. All Saints' Church had two curates to cope with the heavy workload, and it was here that Patrick made his lasting friendship with William Morgan, his fellow curate. Here, too, in the adjacent town of Madely he met the widow of John Fletcher, the great Evangelical preacher, friend of the Wesley brothers, who had been vicar there. Fletcher's house had become a meeting-place for those young clergy who, like Patrick, were of the Evangelical persuasion, and it is clear that he found support and encouragement there. Another important friend from his time in Wellington was John Fennell; it was his niece by marriage, Maria Branwell, whom Patrick was later to marry.

Although Patrick stayed in Wellington for less than a year, this was a very important time for him, both personally and professionally.

DEWSBURY AND HARTSHEAD

Patrick was drawn to his next curacy at All Saints' Church, Dewsbury particularly because the West Riding of Yorkshire, where the town was situated, was at the time the hub of the Wesleyan revival. Here Patrick, encouraged by his vicar, John Buckworth, threw himself into parish work – visiting the sick and the needy, teaching in the Sunday school, preaching and performing baptisms, marriages and funerals. Juliet Barker records how "from October 1810 to February 1811 there were over fifty a month, peaking at seventy-three in November when, on two occasions, there were eight burials in one day." She attributes the steep increase to an outbreak of typhus or influenza, and adds, "There was immense hardship at this time, the failure of the harvest adding to the problems of industrial depression and unemployment."

Patrick's stay at Dewsbury was not long. Fifteen months after his arrival he moved to Hartshead, five miles away. It was during his days at Hartshead that Patrick came into close contact with the Luddites who were protesting violently against the introduction of machinery into the local mills. His stories of the battle

between mill-owners and mill-workers were to make such an impression on Charlotte that she remembered them vividly in her novel *Shirley*.

It was while he was curate of Hartshead that Patrick met and married Maria, and that their two eldest children, Maria and Elizabeth, were born.

THORNTON

Patrick and Maria moved to Thornton with their two young daughters in May 1815, a month before the long wars with France finally ended. The Reverend Thomas Atkinson, perpetual curate of Thornton, wanted to move nearer to his fiancée in Huddersfield and suggested that he and Patrick exchange livings. Patrick was happy to do so, particularly as Thornton had links with Bradford, with which he had already developed close ties; the move also provided him with an increased salary and a house, both important considerations for a man with a young family.

It was here at Thornton that the four younger children were born; and here, too, that the Brontës enjoyed a full and happy social life with the Firth family, who lived nearby, and their circle of friends. Though his next post was a promotion and promised more money and a better house, it must have been with some reluctance that they agreed to leave Thornton. The move, of course, although they wouldn't have known it then, was to be their last – five miles across the moors to Haworth.

ENTRIES IN THE PARISH REGISTER AT THORNTON, SHOWING CHARLOTTE'S BAPTISM IN 1816 AND EMILY'S IN 1818.

THE PARSONAGE
AT HAWORTH

THE DINING ROOM AT
HAWORTH PARSONAGE.
ALL THE FURNITURE
BELONGED TO THE
BRONTËS, BUT SOME
OF IT – LIKE
THE TABLE – DATES
FROM CHARLOTTE'S
LAST YEARS. EMILY
DIED – ACCORDING
TO LEGEND – ON
THE BLACK SOFA
PICTURED HERE.

WHEN PATRICK WAS FINALLY appointed Perpetual Curate to Haworth in February 1820, it was after months of wrangling between the Vicar of Bradford and the Haworth Trustees, whose approval for the appointment had not been sought. Indeed, Patrick, anxious not to be caught in the middle of such an unseemly conflict, had already resigned the curacy before finally accepting it when a compromise was reached.

Of his move to Haworth, Patrick wrote in his diary, "My salary is not large; it is only about £200 a year. I have a good house, which is mine also, and is rent-free." The "good house" was to become home to his six small children, the silent witness to all their imaginings and remarkable creativity – as well as to their tragedies. Set at the top of the village, above the church and backing onto the moor, it stands enveloped on two sides by the churchyard, a constant reminder to the inhabitants of their mortality.

The house itself is a plain, rectangular Georgian building, built in 1778–9. It stands today much as it did in the time of the Brontës, although a gable wing to the right of the house was added after Patrick's death, and minor alterations to the inside were made at that time. It is a surprisingly small house for such a large family. Downstairs to the left of the stone-flagged entrance is the "dining room", or the family living room, in which the sisters worked and wrote, walking round the table discussing and reading out to each other what they had written. Across the passage from the dining room is Patrick's study. At the back of the house downstairs are the kitchen and a small room which was originally a store-room, almost certainly for fuel; at one point, according to legend, it housed the Brontës' pet geese, Adelaide and Victoria, and it was later made into Mr Nicholls' study. The kitchen would have been a hive of activity, the warmest place in the house, where all the family cooking and baking were done, and where the children listened to the servants' gossip and stories.

We do not know exactly where all the inhabitants of the house slept. There are two double bedrooms at the

front of the house, and a tiny room between them which was the children's study but is more often associated with Emily – one of her diary papers shows a sketch of her in this room, her dog Keeper at her feet. Mr Brontë's bedroom looks out on the church and churchyard; it is the room he shared with Branwell during the last years of his son's life. The distress for both of them must have been excruciating: the father watching over him as Branwell succumbed to the addiction of both drink and drugs; Branwell, no doubt, in spite of his own misery, only too aware of how he had failed his father's hopes for him.

The other front bedroom was occupied first by Aunt Branwell (Maria's sister) and then, after Charlotte's marriage, by herself and Mr Nicholls. At the back of the house are a small servants' bedroom and a larger room, which was probably occupied by the girls when they were growing up and later, at one stage, by Branwell as a studio. When the house was full, it is likely that Branwell had to share a room with his father even as a boy and young man, and the girls probably shared beds as well as rooms, as was the custom in large families.

THE MOST DAINTY ORDER

Mrs Gaskell describes rather excessively the Parsonage as she knew it in the 1850s, when Charlotte and Patrick were living alone there with two servants:

> *Everything about the place tells of the most dainty order, the most exquisite cleanliness. The doorsteps are spotless; the small old-fashioned window-panes glitter like looking-glass. Inside and outside of that house cleanliness goes up into its essence, purity.*

All the downstairs rooms had flagstone floors, and for most of the Brontës' time at the Parsonage there were few carpets to absorb the cold. No wonder Aunt Branwell wore her pattens over her shoes indoors! Mr Brontë had an obsessive fear of fire – perhaps wisely

Haworth Church and Parsonage
Published by Smith Elder & Cᵒ 65 Cornhill London 1857

MRS GASKELL'S DRAWING OF HAWORTH CHURCH AND PARSONAGE.

with so many young children in the house – and he would not allow curtains at the windows or, presumably, much in the way of floor coverings. In the bitter Yorkshire winters, the family must have been very glad that the rooms were small and comparatively easy to heat.

THE HEARTH OF HOME

Whatever the discomforts of life at the Parsonage, there is no doubt that it was a much-loved, stable and secure home for all the Brontës. Emily, who hated being away from it, expressed what they all felt:

> *There is a spot mid barren hills*
> *Where winter howls and driving rain,*
> *But if the dreary tempest chills*
> *There is a light that warms again.*
>
> *The house is old, the trees are bare*
> *And moonless bends the misty dome*
> *But what on earth is half so dear,*
> *So longed for as the hearth of home?*

THE PARSONAGE AT HAWORTH

CHARLOTTE

W E KNOW VERY much more about Charlotte than we do about Branwell, Emily or Anne. This is not just because she outlived the last of her siblings by nearly six years, and during that time enjoyed worldwide renown; it is also because, as the eldest remaining child after the deaths of Maria and Elizabeth, she played a dominant role in the family and also made lasting relationships outside it.

Charlotte assumed the mantle of mother to the remaining Brontë children in June 1825, when she was nine years old. For her the sudden deaths of her two older sisters must have been a painful reminder of the earlier loss of her mother, whose place in all their affections had largely been taken by their oldest sister, Maria. From that summer of 1825, Charlotte, Branwell, Emily and Anne were to remain together at the Parsonage, taught by Patrick and Aunt Branwell, and free to explore and create the imaginative worlds of their juvenilia. Charlotte played a very important role in these activities; indeed, she served her apprenticeship as a writer during this time, as did her siblings.

CHARLOTTE'S SCHOOLDAYS

In January 1831, when she was nearly fifteen, Charlotte resumed her formal schooling at Miss Margaret Wooler's School at Roe Head. Mary Taylor, Charlotte's fellow pupil and friend, described her arriving at the school:

> I first saw her coming out of a covered cart, in very old-fashioned clothes, and looking very cold and miserable. She was coming to school at Miss Wooler's. When she appeared in the schoolroom, her dress was changed, but just as old. She looked a little old woman, so short-sighted that she always appeared to be seeking something, and moving her head from side to side to catch a sight of it. She was very shy and nervous, and spoke with a strong Irish accent.

Mary Taylor and her classmates were soon to learn that they had among them an outstanding student:

PORTRAIT OF CHARLOTTE, BY J.H. THOMPSON, A FRIEND OF BRANWELL.

She would confound us by knowing things that were out of our range altogether. She was acquainted with most of the short pieces of poetry that we had to learn by heart … She used to draw much better, and more quickly, than anything we had seen before, and knew much about celebrated pictures and painters … She made poetry and drawing at least exceedingly interesting to me.

In spite of a seemingly inauspicious start, her lack of charm and physical attraction, Charlotte blossomed at Roe Head, winning three prizes at the end of her first year there. More importantly, she made two close and lasting friendships while she was at the school – with Mary Taylor and Ellen Nussey.

Mary Taylor's description of Charlotte's arrival brings to our notice her lack of confidence, her short-sightedness, her ignorance of or inattention to fashion and, puzzlingly, her Irish accent. Where could Charlotte, who had lived all her life in Yorkshire, have got an Irish accent? We can only conclude that, in the isolation of the Parsonage, her father's strong northern brogue and the accents of his Irish curates were the most dominant form of speech she heard.

Such was Charlotte's success as a pupil at Roe Head that she returned there as teacher in 1835. Nineteen years later, when her father could not bring himself to attend her wedding, Charlotte was to ask Miss Wooler to give her away in his place. The years after Roe Head were spent either at the Parsonage or as a governess, except for her first year at the Pensionnat Heger in Brussels, when Charlotte once again became a pupil. As she had done at Roe Head, she went back there as teacher.

THE MATURE NOVELS

Her productive years as a novelist were all spent at Haworth, following the death of Aunt Branwell, when her aunt's bequest to the three girls meant they had some financial security at last. By that time, Charlotte had acquired, through emotional experience, enough material for more than one novel: her Brussels years

were to furnish her with plots and characters, incidents and relationships for *The Professor, Jane Eyre* and *Villette*.

Her writing was, indeed, to be her main strength and consolation in the lonely years that lay ahead after the deaths of Emily and Anne. Not only was it a vehicle for the expression of her suffering, but it occupied her time and it proved an entrée into the London literary world.

When she was thirty-eight, Charlotte married her husband's curate, Arthur Bell Nicholls, who had long been a suitor for her hand. The marriage, a happy one, lasted only nine months; Charlotte died on March 31, 1855. The cause of death entered on the death certificate was "Phthisis", a term used to describe a progressive wasting condition, particularly tuberculosis. According to modern medical opinion, however, her death was more likely to have been from exhaustion caused by extreme nausea in the early stages of pregnancy. On hearing the news, Mrs Gaskell wrote:

I cannot tell you how VERY sad your note has made me. My dear dear friend that I shall never see again on earth! I did not even know she was ill … strangers might know her by her great fame, but we loved her dearly for her goodness, truth, and kindness, & those lovely qualities she carried with her where she is gone.

CHARLOTTE'S WRITING DESK. THE GLASSES ARE A REMINDER THAT SHE WAS VERY SHORT SIGHTED.

BRANWELL

The removal of our only brother must necessarily be regarded by us rather in the light of a mercy than a chastisement. Branwell was his father's and his sisters' pride and hope in boyhood, but since manhood the case has been otherwise.

S O WROTE CHARLOTTE to her editor, William Smith Williams, after Branwell's death at the age of thirty-one, a year younger than Charlotte.

Branwell had been the inspiration for much of the juvenilia, and had been Charlotte's closest collaborator.

SELF-PORTRAIT OF BRANWELL, WHO OFTEN CARICATURED HIMSELF IN HIS DRAWINGS.

Together they had shared the world of the Young Men and Angria, vying with each other in creating and developing the characters and events that were to dominate their childhood. Branwell's "wrong bent" and "the sudden early obscure close of what might have been a noble career" were bitter blows to Charlotte's ambitions for him. Had she not written to Aunt Branwell, "I want us all to go on"?

ARTISTIC PROMISE

Branwell had shown much early promise: sensitive, imaginative, intelligent, he not only wrote the plays and stories of the world he shared with his sisters; like them, he drew and painted and wrote poetry, much of it inspired by or part of his Angrian stories. Unlike the girls, he never went away to school, being educated by his father at the Parsonage. He grew up with a sound knowledge of the classics, a love of music, and the ambition to be both a published poet and a portrait painter. He made repeated efforts to persuade *Blackwood's Magazine* to publish his poetry – without success, although a number of his poems were published in local papers such as the *Bradford Herald* and the *Halifax Guardian*. Indeed, he was the first of the Brontë children to have anything published – a poem in the *Halifax Guardian* in 1841.

The career of portrait painter, for which Branwell seemed destined in his late teens, was never realized; he was, in fact, better at drawing than at painting, as Jane Sellars has pointed out. Nevertheless, he did spend nearly a year in a studio in Bradford, and some portraits of his exist from this time.

THE DOWNWARD SPIRAL

Having failed to make a success of portrait painting, and spurred on by the necessity to earn a living, Branwell went first as tutor to the Postlethwaite family at Broughton in Furness, only to be dismissed six months later. Juliet Barker suggests that he fathered a child there – a child who died some six years later, inspiring Branwell's poem "Epistle from a Father on Earth to his Child in her Grave", published in the *Halifax Guardian* in April 1846.

Whatever the reason for his dismissal from Broughton House, Branwell seems to have started on the unsuccessful path he was to follow for the rest of his life. A brief spell as assistant clerk-in-charge at Sowerby Bridge Railway Station led to promotion the following year to clerk-in-charge of Luddenden Foot Railway Station near Halifax, but a year later he was dismissed from that post, "convicted of constant and culpable carelessness". Although he was not accused or found guilty of any dishonesty there, money was missing and he, as clerk-in-charge, was deemed irresponsible and, therefore, culpable.

Branwell's last post was the most disastrous of all. His sister Anne had already been governess to the Robinson family at Thorp Green near York for two years when Branwell joined her as tutor to the Robinson boys. There he fell in love with the mistress of the house, Lydia Robinson, the wife of his employer, the Reverend Edmund Robinson. It seems likely that she not only reciprocated Branwell's affections, but, his senior by fifteen years, even invited them. It was two and a half years later that Branwell received a letter from Mr Robinson dismissing him for "proceedings ... bad beyond expression". Exactly what prompted Mr Robinson's action is not known.

ALCOHOL AND OPIUM

Branwell was inconsolable. He went into a spiral of despair, blotting out his misery with alcohol and opium. We do not have to look beyond the Parsonage walls to

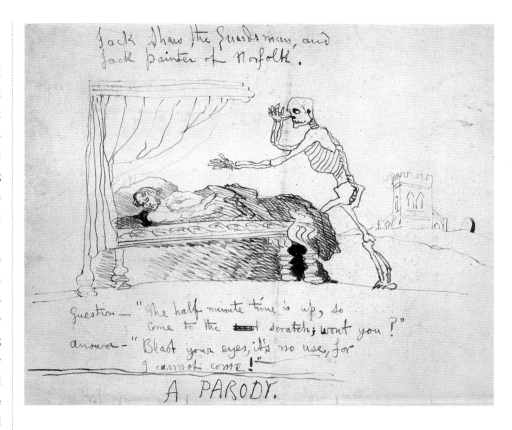

see where Emily learned enough about the effects of alcohol to create Hindley in *Wuthering Heights* or Anne found a model for Helen Graham's husband in *The Tenant of Wildfell Hall*. The sisters witnessed the steady, uncontrolled decline of their brother before their eyes, with all its attendant misery and degradation. For the last months of his life, Branwell shared a bedroom with his father, so that Patrick could watch over him. By the time he died there was no room or energy for "normal" grief. As Charlotte said:

I do not weep from a sense of bereavement – there is no prop withdrawn, no consolation torn away, no dear companion lost – but for the wreck of talent, the ruin of promise, the untimely dreary extinction of what might have been a burning and a shining light. My brother was a year my junior. I had aspirations and ambitions for him once, long ago – they have perished mournfully. Nothing remains of him but a memory of errors and sufferings. There is such a bitterness of pity for his life and death, such a yearning for the emptiness of his whole existence as I cannot describe. I trust time will allay these feelings.

BRANWELL'S SKETCH "A PARODY", IN WHICH HE IS BEING SUMMONED FROM HIS BED BY DEATH.

BRANWELL

EMILY

FRAGMENT OF A
PORTRAIT OF EMILY
BY BRANWELL.

In Emily's nature the extremes of vigour and simplicity seemed to meet. Under an unsophisticated culture … and an unpretending outside, lay a secret power and fire that might have informed the brain and kindled the veins of a hero; but she had no worldly wisdom; her powers were unadapted to the practical business of life … An interpreter ought always to have stood between her and the world …

S O WROTE CHARLOTTE in a biographical notice to her sisters' work after their deaths. As Juliet Barker points out, Charlotte had one aim in mind: "to answer the critics who had complained of 'Ellis' and 'Acton's' love of the coarse, brutal and degrading." She goes on to say that "Charlotte built the edifice under which the Brontës have sheltered ever since."

How far is this a true picture of Emily and how much a portrait of the sister Charlotte wanted the world to see and know? How much does it reflect Charlotte's own need to be the interpreter between her sisters and the world?

Unsophisticated Emily certainly was not, if by that term we mean uncomplicated, lacking in subtlety or cultivation. We know, however, that in many ways she must have appeared so to people outside the family. Her extreme reticence often made her seem rude, unresponding and socially inept, which no doubt she was; her mode of dress was both eccentric and unattractive, particularly the dresses with leg-of-mutton sleeves that she persisted in wearing long after they were out of fashion. When teased by her fellow pupils in Brussels she responded with, "I wish to be as God made me." To respond so requires, of course, both courage and an independence of mind that Emily clearly had:

No coward soul is mine,
No trembler in the world's storm-troubled sphere

she declares in one of her poems. Nobody reading either her poems or *Wuthering Heights* would doubt that she did, indeed, possess "a secret power and fire that might have informed the brain and kindled the veins of a hero." Monsieur Heger had said of her: "She should have been a man – a great navigator … her strong, imperious will would never have been daunted by opposition or difficulty; never have given way but with life."

A STRONG, IMPERIOUS WILL

There are several stories that support this view of her. In *Shirley* Charlotte describes an incident, which Mrs Gaskell says was suggested by an identical event in Emily's life. She had befriended an unknown dog, which had bitten her. Aware of the danger of rabies, she went immediately into the Parsonage kitchen and cauterized the wound herself with a red-hot iron. On another occasion, according to Mrs Gaskell, she beat her own dog, Keeper, whom she loved dearly, with her bare fists because he had transgressed the rules of the Parsonage by sleeping on one of the beds. We have only to read Charlotte's accounts of her sister's death at the age of thirty from tuberculosis to realize that Emily possessed extraordinary self-control and willpower:

> She sank rapidly. She made haste to leave us. Yet, while physically she perished, mentally, she grew stronger than we had yet known her. Day by day, when I saw with what a front she met suffering, I looked on her with an anguish of wonder and love. I have seen nothing like it; but, indeed, I have never seen her parallel in anything. Stronger than a man, simpler than a child, her nature stood alone.

When Charlotte writes of Anne, she does so in a simple, straightforward, uncomplicated way; in contrast, there is always something of the mysterious, the inexplicable, the awe-inspiring, the dramatic – even melodramatic – in her references to Emily.

If Emily is homesick while at school at Roe Head, then Charlotte is sure she will die unless she goes home. It is clear that this sister of hers had a special power of which Charlotte was very aware. Readers of *Wuthering Heights* are very aware of it, too.

Yet Emily's powers were not, as Charlotte said in the biographical notice, wholly "unadapted to the practical business of life". It was she, for instance, who took on the task of family housekeeper after Aunt Branwell's death, and we know that she shared fully in the daily routine chores at the Parsonage.

It was at home that Emily was happiest. "My sister Emily loved the moors", wrote Charlotte, and Mrs Gaskell relates how, when Emily was dying in December 1848, Charlotte went in search of one sprig of late-flowering heather to bring to her sister. On returning, she saw that Emily was already too near death to recognize it. Charlotte's anguish at her loss is expressed in the passionate and lyrical account she wrote to Smith Williams:

> Emily is nowhere here now – her wasted mortal remains are taken out of the house; we have laid her cherished head under the church-aisle beside my mother's, my two sisters', dead long ago, and my poor, hapless brother's …

> Well – the loss is ours – not hers, and some sad comfort I take, as I hear the wind blow and feel the cutting keenness of the frost, in knowing that the elements bring her no more suffering – their severity cannot reach her grave – her fever is quieted, her restlessness soothed, her deep, hollow cough is hushed for ever …

EMILY'S
CHRISTENING MUG.

DIARY PAPER
SHOWING EMILY
WITH KEEPER
AT HER SIDE.

ANNE

Anne, dear gentle Anne, was quite different in appearance from the others. She was her aunt's favourite. Her hair was a very pretty, light brown, and fell on her neck in graceful curls. She had lovely violet-blue eyes, fine pencilled eyebrows, and clear, almost transparent complexion.

So wrote Ellen Nussey, Charlotte's friend from their days together at Roe Head, of the youngest of the Brontë sisters. It is this picture of "dear gentle Anne" that has come down to us through the years. Elizabeth Gaskell, describing the portrait Branwell painted of his sisters, writes:

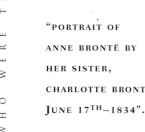

The picture was divided, almost in the middle, by a great pillar. On the side of the column which was lighted by the sun, stood Charlotte, in the womanly dress of that day of gigot sleeves and large collars. On the deeply shadowed side, was Emily, with Anne's gentle face resting on her shoulder. Emily's countenance struck me as full of power; Charlotte's of solicitude; Anne's of tenderness ... I remember looking on those two sad, earnest, shadowed faces, and wondering whether I could trace the mysterious expression which is said to foretell an early death.

"PORTRAIT OF ANNE BRONTË BY HER SISTER, CHARLOTTE BRONTË, JUNE 17TH–1834".

Readers of *The Tenant of Wildfell Hall* must surely wonder how such a "gentle" woman could create such a powerful and violent novel.

Anne was only three months old when the family moved to Haworth, and twenty months old when her mother died. Asthmatic and delicate, she, more than any of the other children, grew up under the care and direction of Aunt Branwell. Unlike her sisters, she never went to the Clergy Daughters' School but was taught at home the accomplishments she would need to earn her living in the world as a teacher or governess. It was inevitable that her aunt would have a profound influence on Anne's development, but it is difficult to know just how much the spiritual conflict of her later years was initiated by Aunt Branwell's religious zeal.

Whatever the source, Anne's religious faith and her struggle to reconcile traditional views of good and evil, heaven and hell with her own merciful and compassionate nature were to dominate her life. Like the poet, William Cowper, she suffered from periods of acute religious melancholy in which she feared she could not possibly merit salvation. It is this preoccupation with eternal salvation that dominates the last stages of Helen Huntingdon's marriage in *The Tenant of Wildfell Hall*. Her one concern is that her drunken, violent, abusive husband should not enter eternity unrepentant and risk the damnation of his soul.

ANNE AND EMILY

Anne's closest companion in the family was Emily: "She and Anne were like twins – inseparable companions, and in the very closest sympathy, which never had any interruption," Ellen Nussey wrote of them when Anne was thirteen and Emily fifteen. It was they who exchanged diary papers and created Gondal together. It was, in many ways, a natural alliance: the two youngest siblings, dominated by Charlotte and Branwell and their world, found their own identities in a shared rejection of Angria. Certainly, the world of Gondal owes much to their common love of nature in all its moods and manifestations.

Anne's poetry, like Emily's, is full of the images which surrounded them on the moors: hills, trees, birds, sky, wind. It is tempting to think that Emily's pantheistic nature and rejection of traditional Christian morality was a healthy antidote to Anne's more disturbing conventional beliefs.

EDUCATION
AND OCCUPATION

At the age of sixteen Anne went away from home for the first time: she joined Charlotte, who was now teaching at Roe Head School, taking Emily's place as a pupil, and experiencing the only two years she was to have of formal education. Unlike Emily and Charlotte, she did not go to Brussels to acquire the accomplishments considered necessary for them as teachers, probably because she was already employed as a governess by that time.

It was during the last four years of Anne's life that the sisters published their book of poems, and she wrote her two novels. As Brussels provided the raw material for most of Charlotte's fiction, Anne's positions as governess gave her the experience and insight to write *Agnes Grey*. The seeds of *The Tenant of Wildfell Hall* are more difficult to identify, although it is not difficult to see where some of her preoccupations in the novel have come from.

Anne survived Emily by only five months. Within a month of Emily's death, Anne's tuberculosis was diagnosed as fatal. Unlike Emily, she cooperated with doctors trying to treat her throughout the final months of her life, but her imminent end was never really in any doubt. Anne had a special love of the sea, which she had enjoyed for several summers when, as a governess, she accompanied the Robinson family to Scarborough on the Yorkshire coast. It was to this seaside resort that she,

Charlotte and Ellen Nussey travelled, in a last, vain attempt to prolong Anne's life. She died there on May 28, 1849 at the age of just twenty-nine. Charlotte wrote to Smith Williams,

She died without severe struggle, resigned, trusting in God – thankful for release from a suffering life – deeply assured that a better existence lay before her. She believed, she hoped – and declared her belief and hope with her last breath.

Anxious to spare her father another funeral, Charlotte decided that Anne should be buried at Scarborough. She lies there now – the only one of the Brontë family not in the vault at Haworth – overlooking the sea.

ANNE'S GRAVE AT SCARBOROUGH. THE AGE ON THE HEAD-STONE IS WRONG, SHE WAS, IN FACT, 29 WHEN SHE DIED.

ANNE

ELIZABETH BRANWELL

WHEN ELIZABETH BRANWELL arrived from Cornwall to look after her sister Maria and the six Brontë children in the spring of 1821, she can hardly have expected that she would spend the rest of her life in the dour Yorkshire township.

Maria was dying of cancer – slowly and painfully – and all the children had had scarlet fever. Patrick was struggling to keep up his parish work and look after his ill family with the help of their servants and a nurse called in to tend to Mrs Brontë. He was very conscious of his isolation, having so recently moved to Haworth from Thornton; "a stranger in a strange land", he called himself. It would have been, one imagines, a great relief

**SILHOUETTE OF
AUNT BRANWELL.**

to him at such a time that a close relative of his wife should join the family, both sharing his parental and household responsibilities and providing him with adult companionship. Indeed, he was later to say as much, relating how his sister-in-law "afforded great comfort to my mind, which has been the case ever since, by sharing my labours and sorrows, and behaving as an affectionate mother to my children."

Elizabeth Branwell must, one suspects, have had some misgivings about the task she was taking on, although there was no suggestion at that stage, of course, that it would be a lifetime's work. She had come to help the family out at a difficult time, although it must have occurred to Elizabeth that her stay might be a prolonged one as it was already obvious that Maria was not going to recover.

Elizabeth Branwell was already well known to Patrick since she had lived with the Brontë family at Thornton for over a year; during that time she had become godmother to their second daughter, Elizabeth. As Juliet Barker says, Patrick's own comments about her – "sharing my labours and sorrows" and "an affectionate mother to my children" – serve as a healthy reminder to readers that Mrs Gaskell's interpretation of life at the Parsonage and the people who lived there is not always an accurate one. She begins Chapter IV of her biography of Charlotte by saying that Miss Branwell arrived "About a year after Mrs Bronte's death", which we know is not true, and goes on to say:

> Miss Branwell was, I believe, a kindly and conscientious woman, with a good deal of character, but with the some-what narrow ideas natural to one who had spent nearly

all her life in the same place. She had strong prejudices, and soon took a dislike to Yorkshire … The children respected her, and had that sort of affection for her which is generated by esteem; but I do not think they ever freely loved her.

It is clear that Aunt Branwell found Yorkshire and its climate both strange and hostile and looked back with nostalgia to the more halcyon days of her youth in Cornwall. Both Mrs Gaskell and Ellen Nussey report her wearing pattens over her shoes to protect her feet from the cold of the Parsonage flagstones, and Ellen remembers her talking "a great deal of her younger days." As Mrs Gaskell says, "It was a severe trial for anyone at her time of life to change neighbourhood and habitation so entirely as she did, and the greater her merit."

Whether Mrs Gaskell was right and the children never "freely loved her", we shall probably never know; but certainly she provided for them the stable female figure they would otherwise have lacked. Branwell wrote at her death in 1842, "I have now lost the guide and director of all the happy days connected with my childhood." Elizabeth Branwell would surely have run her brother-in-law's household efficiently, disciplined the children effectively – as Anne's and Emily's diary papers show, and, as Patrick says, provided adult company for him.

Mrs Gaskell says "I do not know whether Miss Branwell taught her nieces anything besides sewing, and the household arts in which Charlotte afterwards was such an adept. Their regular lessons were said to their father." While this is probably generally true, it is unlikely that Patrick took charge of his daughters' lessons until they could at least read and write. Presumably, the rudiments of their education were left to Aunt Branwell to instill. It is interesting to imagine what she would have thought of their atrocious spelling and punctuation!

In practical terms the sisters had much to thank Aunt Branwell for. Charlotte's and Emily's time in Brussels was made possible by her generosity. When they wanted to set up a school of their own in the Parsonage, Charlotte approached their aunt for help with furthering their education so that they would be better equipped to run their own establishment. Aunt Branwell agreed to let them have fifty pounds for the venture. And her bequest, on her death, to Charlotte, Emily and Anne granted them at least a modicum of financial independence. To Branwell, ironically, she left no money: he was expected, as a young man, to be able to make his own way in the world.

THE EVERLASTING FIRE

Aunt Branwell, like her sister Maria, was brought up a Wesleyan Methodist, and the Brontë biographer Winifred Gérin certainly lays at her door responsibility for Anne's religious crises:

To Aunt Branwell the Everlasting Fire was a furnace of very real substance and combustible power; the likelihood of an infant falling into it was just as great as of her falling into the nursery fire … Hell was very real and damnation certain for the vast majority of mankind. To seek to turn away from everlasting perdition the persons committed to one's care … was the whole duty of a Christian gentlewoman.

Juliet Barker disagrees with Winifred Gérin's picture of Aunt Branwell, finding little or no evidence to support this view of her. Evangelical by persuasion, like her brother-in-law, she seems to have adapted perfectly happily to the Church of England, of which – like Maria – she became a member. She was buried, with her adopted family, in the vault of Haworth Church.

SMELLING SALT BOTTLES BELONGING TO THE BRANWELL SISTERS.

SCHOOLDAYS

ALL THAT REMAINS TODAY OF THE CLERGY DAUGHTERS' SCHOOL AT COWAN BRIDGE.

WHEN PATRICK DECIDED to send his young daughters to the Clergy Daughters' School at Cowan Bridge, some fifty miles from Haworth, there was no doubt that he thought he was providing well for them. Maria and Elizabeth had already spent a short time at Crofton Hall near Wakefield, but Patrick could not continue to pay their expensive fees as well as educate his younger daughters.

Juliet Barker quotes the advertisement in the *Leeds Intelligencer* for the new Clergy Daughters' School stipulating that "every Effort will be made to confine the Benefits of the School to the *really* necessitous Clergy, and especially to those who are the most exemplary in their Life and Doctrine". It must have sounded encour-

aging to the father of five daughters, for whom a sound education was essential if they were to make their way in the world. "… each Girl is to pay £14 a Year (Half in Advance) for Clothing, Lodging, Boarding, and Education", read the advertisement,

> *… and £1 Entrance towards the Expense of Books, &c. The Education will be directed according to the Capacities of the Pupils, and the Wishes of their Friends. In all Cases, the great Object in View will be their intellectual and religious Improvement …*

Whatever doubts Patrick may have had about sending his young daughters away to school, he must have overcome them, for in July 1824 his two eldest daughters, Maria and Elizabeth, entered the Clergy Daughters' School, to be followed in August by Charlotte, and in November by Emily – she was just six years old.

COWAN BRIDGE AND JANE EYRE

There is no doubt that Charlotte's descriptions of life at Lowood in *Jane Eyre* are taken from her experiences at Cowan Bridge, as Mrs Gaskell records:

> *Miss Brontë more than once said to me, that she should not have written what she did of Lowood in* Jane Eyre*, if she thought the place would have been so immediately identified with Cowan Bridge, although there was not a word in her account of the institution but what was true at the time when she knew it.*

Charlotte had gone on to say, however, that "in a work of fiction", she did not feel obliged to "state every particular with the impartiality that might be required in a court of justice." Readers of *Jane Eyre* have been inclined to treat the fiction as fact and attribute to Carus Wilson, the school's head, all the sins of Mr Brocklehurst.

What we know about the school is that it certainly was, like many others of its day, both strict and rigorous in its discipline and daily routine. Long morning prayers preceded breakfast, and the food, if Jane Eyre's descriptions are anything to go by, was both unappetizing and sparse. The children were often cold, and their whole existence was generally without comfort and any of the small luxuries they might have enjoyed at home. Unlike some institutions, however, the school did put considerable emphasis on cleanliness, presumably in an attempt to safeguard the girls' health. Ironically, their efforts were in vain.

LOW FEVER

In the late winter of 1825 – only seven months after Maria's and Elizabeth's arrival at Cowan Bridge – an epidemic of "low fever", or typhus, broke out in the school. Charlotte describes the spread of the disease in *Jane Eyre*,

That forest dell, where Lowood lay, was the cradle of fog and fog-bread pestilence; which ... crept into the Orphan Asylum, breathed typhus through its crowded schoolroom and dormitory, and ... transformed the seminary into a hospital ... Semi-starvation and neglected colds had predisposed most of the pupils to receive infection: forty-five out of the eighty girls lay ill at one time ...

It was from such a situation that Maria, already very ill with consumption, was sent home. Her death in May was followed, three weeks later, by Elizabeth's arrival at the Parsonage. On seeing her, Patrick went at once to Cowan Bridge and collected Charlotte and Emily; Elizabeth died two weeks later. It is hardly surprising that the loss of their two oldest sisters in such circumstances coloured Charlotte's perception of the school. It

was to be a number of years before Patrick would allow his remaining children to venture from home.

When he did so, six years later, it was to send Charlotte to Miss Margaret Wooler's school at Roe Head. Her years there, after a difficult start, were both happy and successful. She impressed both teachers and pupils with her extraordinary breadth of reading, her unusual memory and her creative gifts. So successful was she that, in 1835, she returned there as a teacher. This time Emily accompanied her. She had not been away from the Parsonage since she left Cowan Bridge nearly ten years earlier: the experience was so traumatic that she became physically ill and had to be sent home. Charlotte wrote lyrically of her sister's dilemma:

Liberty was the breath of Emily's nostrils; without it, she perished ... Her nature proved here too strong for her fortitude. Every morning when she woke, the vision of home and the moors rushed on her, and darkened and saddened the day that lay before her. Nobody knew what ailed her but me ... I felt in my heart she would die if she did not go home, and with this conviction obtained her recall.

Emily's place at Roe Head was taken by Anne who, although homesick and unhappy herself, managed better than Emily. She remained at Miss Wooler's school first at Roe Head and then at Dewsbury Moor for two years.

The Brontë sisters needed a formal education to equip them for their lives as governesses and teachers; and there's no doubt that Charlotte benefited from her time at Roe Head and both Charlotte and Emily from the kind of intellectual discipline they learned while in Brussels. It is also quite clear, however, that the most important education they received was from their reading and from each other in the long apprenticeship they served as young writers at the Parsonage.

THE REVEREND CARUS WILSON, THE EVANGELICAL FOUNDER OF THE CLERGY DAUGHTERS' SCHOOL.

SCHOOLDAYS

PAGE 31

SERVANTS
AT HAWORTH

NANCY GARRS, WHO
ACCOMPANIED THE
BRONTË FAMILY
TO HAWORTH.

THE KITCHEN AT THE
BRONTË PARSONAGE
MUSEUM.

THE FACT THAT the Brontës had servants comes as something of a surprise to some modern visitors to the Parsonage. Yet while Patrick was not a wealthy man, it would have been unthinkable for somebody in his position not to employ help in running the household. Manual work, particularly that done by women, was, of course, very cheap – a few pounds a year with board would have been the average servant girl's remuneration, well within Patrick's budget.

NANCY AND SARAH GARRS

In 1816, when Maria Brontë had three children under three to look after, the Brontës engaged a thirteen-year old girl, Nancy Garrs, as nursery maid. After the birth of Emily she was made cook and assistant housekeeper, and her younger sister, Sarah, appointed nursemaid. Both girls were to prove most loyal servants, moving with the family from Thornton to Haworth and seeing them all through the very difficult years of Mrs Brontë's illness and death. Indeed, they left the Parsonage only months before the deaths of Maria and Elizabeth.

It was to be the evidence of the Garrs, with their intimate knowledge of the family and life at the Parsonage, that contradicted many of the more exaggerated and melodramatic stories which Mrs Gaskell related in her first editions of *The Life of Charlotte Brontë*. From the accounts we have, it can be seen that the two young servant girls were treated as members of the family and became both friends and companions of the Brontë children.

TABITHA AYKROYD

The best known and the best loved of the Brontë servants was, undoubtedly, Tabitha Aykroyd. She came to the Parsonage as cook early in 1825 and was to remain with the family for thirty years. Such was the affection they all felt for her that, when she fell, breaking a leg, the sisters insisted on looking after her for, as Charlotte wrote to Ellen Nussey, "she was like one of our own family". When the leg later became badly ulcerated and Tabitha was forced to leave the Parsonage for a while, Charlotte again wrote to Ellen:

She is very comfortable and wants nothing. As she is near we see her very often – In the meantime Emily and I are sufficiently busy as you may suppose – I manage the iron-ing and keep the rooms clean – Emily does the baking and attends to the Kitchen – We are such odd animals that we prefer this mode of contrivance to having a new face among us. Besides we do not despair of Tabby's return and she shall not be supplanted by a stranger in her absence.

By the end of 1842, Tabitha was back at the Parsonage, joined by Martha Brown, the young daughter of John Brown, sexton of Haworth Church and Branwell's friend.

These two servants were to follow Branwell and Emily to their graves and receive Charlotte as she returned from Scarborough after the death of Anne. Tabitha was to die, at the age of eighty-four, only six weeks before Charlotte; she is buried just over the wall from the Parsonage garden, beside the path which would, in the Brontës' time, have led directly from their front door to the church – the path which all of them, except Anne, would have taken to their final resting place. Martha, too, is buried in Haworth churchyard. After Patrick's death, she agreed to go as a servant to Arthur Bell Nicholls' home in Ireland; but by late 1862 she was back in Haworth where she stayed apart from the occasional holiday in Ireland. Mr Nicholls' attempts to persuade her to remain with them were in vain, as his letter of March 1868 shows:

I fear Haworth does not agree with you, as it is cold & damp. I wish you could make up your mind to live with us, I don't mean as a servant; but to make this your home …

In the absence of their mother, the presence of Tabitha Aykroyd in particular must have been comfort-

ing and reassuring for the Brontë children. Diary papers and letters show that she was a very important figure in the Parsonage. Not only did she look after their physical well-being, but she was, by all accounts, a solid, emo-tionally stable person in their lives, as well as the source of fascinating stories and village gossip. Where else would the children have learned their Yorkshire dialect? And, surely, she is a likely model for Nelly Dean, the housekeeper-confidante of *Wuthering Heights*?

That the Brontë family inspired and retained the love and loyalty of their servants is a tribute to their con-sideration and loyalty as employers. When Patrick died he left to Martha Brown the sum of thirty pounds, "as a token of regard for long and faithful services to me and my children." And Tabby's gravestone refers to her as the faithful servant of the Brontë family.

MARTHA BROWN, ONE OF THE BRONTË FAMILY'S FAITHFUL SERVANTS.

A LOVE
OF ANIMALS

EMILY'S WATERCOLOUR
OF HER BELOVED AND
DEVOTED DOG,
KEEPER, WHO –
ON EMILY'S DEATH –
JOINED THE
MOURNERS AT
HER FUNERAL AND
"HOWLED PITIFULLY
FOR MANY DAYS".

ALL THE BRONTËS loved animals. We see this love expressed in their drawing and painting, in their letters and in their novels. Among Emily's Brussels essays is one called "Le Chat", in which she shows a characteristically perceptive and intelligent awareness of that animal's nature: "Man", she wrote, "cannot stand up to comparison with the dog; for the dog is infinitely too good", but "the cat, while it differs in certain physical aspects, is very like us in character". Cats and dogs were constant inhabitants of the

Parsonage and companions of the Brontë family. The best known of the dogs were Anne's Flossy and Emily's Keeper, both of whom survived their mistresses. Mrs Gaskell writes movingly, if fancifully, of Keeper after Emily's death:

> [H]e loved her dearly … he walked first among the mourners to her funeral; he slept moaning for nights at the door of her empty room … He, in his turn, was mourned over by the surviving sister. Let us somehow hope, in half Red Indian creed, that he follows Emily now; and, when he rests, sleeps on some soft white bed of dreams, unpunished when he awakens to the life of the land of shadows.

The last sentence, of course, is suggested by the story about Emily punishing Keeper for sleeping on one of the Parsonage beds.

Emily painted both Keeper and Flossy, so we are able to visualize them both very clearly when we read such stories or Charlotte's sensitive and sympathetic account of the dogs' grief at the loss of their owners when she returned from Scarborough without Anne.

Keeper from life April 24 1838 Emily Jane Brontë

TWO GEESE AND A HAWK

It was not just usual household pets, however, that found their way into the Parsonage. There were the two tame geese, Adelaide and Victoria, who reputedly lived for a time in the small back room later to become Mr Nicholls' study, and a hawk, Nero (sometimes wrongly spelt Hero), which they had rescued from the moors. In her July 1845 diary paper, Emily lamented their loss, which she discovered when she returned from Brussels, Aunt Branwell having taken advantage of her absence to get rid of the pets:

We have got Flossey; got and lost Tiger – lost the Hawk. Nero which with the geese was given away and is doubtless dead for when I came back from Brussels I enquired on all hands and could hear nothing of him … Keeper and Flossey are well also the canary acquired 4 years since.

Mrs Gaskell records how Charlotte wrote in a letter, "Our poor little cat has been ill two days, and is just dead. It is piteous to see even an animal lying lifeless. Emily is sorry." And Mrs Gaskell goes on to say, "Charlotte was more than commonly tender in her treatment of all dumb creatures … not merely were her actions kind, her words and tones were ever gentle and caressing, towards animals," and she reminds us that the heroine in *Shirley* judges her lover by his attitude to animals.

In the Brontë novels, the animals, particularly dogs, are memorable. There is Pilot, Mr Rochester's companion, in *Jane Eyre*, and Tartar, modelled on Keeper, in *Shirley*. Agnes Grey speaks of her "affliction" when,

Snap, my little dumb, rough-visaged, but bright-eyed, warm-hearted companion, the only thing I had to love me, was taken away, and delivered over to the tender mercies of the village rat-catcher, a man notorious for his brutal treatment of his canine slaves.

As in *Shirley*, one of the ways in which Agnes' lover shows himself worthy of her love is in his attitude to the unfortunate, mistreated Snap. Strikingly, the dogs in *Wuthering Heights* play an almost symbolic role,

expressed in their names, Gnasher, Wolf, Throttler – paradoxical, perhaps, as the creations of Emily, of whom Mrs Gaskell records an acquaintance saying, "she never showed regard to any human creature; all her love was reserved for animals." When Keeper died, just before the anniversary of Emily's death in December 1851, Charlotte told Ellen Nussey, "There was something very sad in losing the old dog; yet I am glad he met a natural fate; people kept hinting he ought to be put away which neither Papa nor I liked to think of." They "laid his old faithful head in the garden". Flossy's death, too, is recorded, three years later, in a letter to Ellen,

Did I tell you that our poor little Flossy is dead? He drooped for a single day, and died quietly in the night without pain. The loss even of a dog was very saddening; yet perhaps no dog ever had a happier life or an easier death.

EMILY'S WATER-COLOUR OF A MERLIN, PERHAPS INSPIRED BY HER PET HAWK, NERO.

GOVERNESSES

THE POSITION OF WOMEN in the first half of the nineteenth century was much as it had been when Jane Austen was a young woman in the late eighteenth century.

At the bottom end of the social structure, of course, women – whether married or single – have always worked, on farms, in inns, in shops, as household servants, and, later, in the factories. Such women were employed by the Brontës in the Parsonage and by the millowners of Haworth. For those at the top of the social scale, work was not an option: either they married or they remained the responsibility of their fathers all their lives. For women between these two extremes, there were few choices. They could teach in a school or they could go into a large private house as a governess.

Winifred Gérin, in her biography of Elizabeth Gaskell, aptly describes the position of young women like the Gaskell daughters and the Brontë sisters,

If a girl of good family had to earn her living there was little or no choice ... They must go out as governesses to a strange family ... Governessing did not totally rule out hopes of marriage for a girl, as Jane Eyre is there to prove. But Mrs Gaskell dreaded such a fate for her own daughters and it was largely because of this that she was determined to buy a family home which could be inherited in due course by those who failed to marry.

The Brontë sisters had no mother to buy them a family home. The Parsonage belonged to the Church and, on their father's death, would house the new incumbent; they had as much reason to feel insecure as Jane Austen's Bennet daughters. Unlike Mr Bennet, however, Patrick Brontë had tried to ensure that his daughters could support themselves, albeit humbly. Both Anne and Charlotte were to become governesses, neither was happy in the situation.

Governesses were from what we might now call a "middle-class" (sometimes upper-middle-class) background, women whose fathers were in no position to provide for them and had no prospect of doing so. They had enjoyed at least a limited education, which would have included some music, painting and drawing, perhaps a knowledge of a foreign language, together with

sewing and embroidery. This was the education the Brontë sisters themselves had had at the Parsonage and later at school in England and Brussels. It is the lot of women in this position that particularly interests Charlotte and Anne Brontë in their novels; they are the people whose role in life is most like their own.

JANE AND AGNES

Having been both teacher and governess, like her heroine Jane Eyre, Charlotte was aware that neither position offered a woman any real independence and both were very badly paid. The role of the governess was extremely lonely: better educated and of a higher social class than the servants, she was not expected to look for companionship there. She was also regarded as inferior to her employers by the very fact that she needed employment, though in all other respects she was often their equal in upbringing and their superior in education. In *Jane Eyre* Mary and Diana Rivers are forced to go,

> ... as governesses in a large, fashionable, south-of-England city, where each held a situation in families by whose wealthy and haughty members they were regarded only as humble dependants, and who neither knew not sought one of their innate excellences, and appreciated only their acquired accomplishments as they appreciated the skill of their cook or the taste of their waiting-woman.

Jane, of course, fares better: her loneliness at Thornfield is alleviated by her love for Rochester, but her isolation is still very evident. Mrs Fairfax, the housekeeper, advises her on how to join Rochester's distinguished company:

> I'll tell you how to manage so as to avoid the embarrassment of making a formal entrance, which is the most disagreeable part of the business. You must go into the drawing-room while it is empty, before the ladies leave the dinner-table; choose your seat in any quiet nook you like; you need not stay long after the gentlemen come in, unless you please: just let Mr Rochester see you are there and then slip away – nobody will notice you.

Agnes Grey's experiences in the families where she becomes a governess must, one feels, reflect what Anne had observed or experienced in the same role. Agnes tells of parents undermining her authority with the children in her care, of the children's extreme naughtiness and bad manners, not to say their arrogance and stupidity: "it is very unpleasant to live with such unimpressible, incomprehensible creatures. You cannot love them, and if you could, your love would be utterly thrown away; they could neither return it, nor value, nor understand it." And one of her charges, Master Charles, she describes as:

> ... his mother's peculiar darling ... a pettish, cowardly, capricious, selfish little fellow, only active in doing mischief, and only clever in inventing falsehoods, not simply to hide his faults, but, in mere malicious wantonness, to bring odium upon others; in fact, Master Charles was a very great nuisance to me: it was a trial of patience to live with him peaceably; to watch over him was worse; and to teach him, or pretend to teach him, was inconceivable.

It is not surprising that Mrs Gaskell wished to spare her daughters a similar fate and that all three Brontë sisters were so anxious to set up their own school. Their ambition was to be self-supporting and avoid the necessity for any of them to go away as governesses.

JANE EYRE AND HER
PRECOCIOUS
CHARGE, ADÈLE.

THE PENSIONNAT HEGER

I would not go to France or to Paris. I would go to Brussels, in Belgium. The cost of the journey there, at the dearest rate of travelling, would be £5; living is there little more than half as dear as it is in England, and the facilities for education are equal or superior to any other place in Europe. In half a year, I could acquire a thorough familiarity with French. I could improve greatly in Italian, and even get a dash of German …

S O WROTE CHARLOTTE to her Aunt Branwell, going on to say, "Papa will perhaps think it a wild and ambitious scheme; but who ever rose in the world without ambition? When he left Ireland to go to Cambridge University, he was as ambitious as I am now. I want us *all* to go on."

PLAQUE COMMEMORATING THE SITE OF THE NOW DEMOLISHED PENSIONNAT HEGER IN BRUSSELS.

A SCHOOL OF THEIR OWN

Charlotte was appealing for help financially with a scheme very dear to her heart. Faced with the necessity of earning their own livings, the Brontë sisters could look forward only to the drudgery and loneliness of the life of a governess or to the equally onerous life of the teacher in some young ladies' establishment. There was, however, one way of escape from such a future: to set up a school of their own, where they would be in control of their own destinies and where they would be able to live and work together.

In order to attract pupils of a suitable class and background, it was essential that the Brontë sisters offer the kind of curriculum that was required by the parents of young ladies. Their chances of providing this would be greatly enhanced if they could show that they had themselves had a continental education and were proficient in languages.

So it was that, with Aunt Branwell's help of fifty pounds, Charlotte and Emily set out for the Pensionnat Heger in Brussels on February 8, 1842. With them, to escort them on their journey and settle them into their school, went their father, as well as Charlotte's close friend Mary Taylor and her brother Joe.

"NO COWARD SOUL"

What Emily felt about the prospect of six months in a Brussels school we can only imagine. The homesickness she suffered as a pupil at Roe Head in 1835 and a teacher at Miss Patchett's school at Law Hill where she went in 1838 had been so acute that she had remained at neither school more than a few months.

It can only have been the prospect of securing for themselves a future which did not necessitate leaving home that persuaded Emily she must accompany Charlotte to Brussels. Accompany her she did, and stayed not just six months but nine, determined, perhaps, to show that hers was "No coward soul".

Emily impressed her teacher as being the possessor of genius "something even higher" than Charlotte's and clearly made excellent use of her education in Brussels. She appears to have coped with her exile by dedicating herself exclusively to her work and her music – she had lessons from the best music teacher in Brussels and, in the last months of their stay, taught music herself at the school. Yet, so far as we can see, her time abroad made no lasting impression on or difference to Emily's life or to the subject matter of her literary works.

CHARLOTTE'S PASSION

For Charlotte the experience was very different. She cannot have imagined, as she arrived at the Pensionnat Heger, that she was about to meet the man with whom she was to fall passionately and obsessively in love, nor that the experience would provide the material for three of her four novels.

Constantin Heger was the husband of the directrice of the school; he gave Emily and Charlotte their French literature lessons, and he soon discovered the unusual talents of his two English pupils. A stern and demanding taskmaster, Heger encouraged the sisters to discipline their creative and critical gifts, playing a major part in Charlotte's development as a writer. However, it was not simply an intellectual influence which he exerted on her: Charlotte found emotional, as well as intellectual, support in her new teacher.

Emily's and Charlotte's stay was extended beyond the six months originally agreed and was ended after nine months only when, in November 1842, they received the news that Aunt Branwell had been taken ill. The sisters returned to Haworth to find she had already died. Emily remained at home, in charge of the housekeeping at the Parsonage and in order to take care of her father, but Charlotte returned alone to Brussels in January 1843, this time as a teacher at the Pensionnat Heger.

It must very soon have become obvious to both the Hegers that Charlotte had become passionately attached to Monsieur Heger. From this time Charlotte's attitude to his wife became increasingly critical and her letters to friends constantly bewailed her isolation and loneliness, as Monsieur Heger withdrew from what must have felt to him like a persecutory obsession. It is in her novel *Villette* and in her subsequent letters to Monsieur Heger that she expresses most effectively and poignantly her feelings for him.

Charlotte finally left Brussels in January 1844 to return to Haworth. It would be difficult to overestimate the importance of the time she spent there and its influence on her creative life.

GARDEN OF THE PENSIONNAT HEGER, IN THE 1840S, AS EMILY AND CHARLOTTE WOULD PROBABLY HAVE KNOWN IT.

FRIENDS AND COMPANIONS

IT IS HARDLY SURPRISING that, of all the Brontë children, Charlotte and Branwell made the most important friendships outside the family circle. While the children were together at the Parsonage, following the deaths of Maria and Elizabeth, they were, in many ways, emotionally self-sufficient. As Branwell, the only boy, grew older, however, he naturally looked outside the home for masculine companionship, and it was when Charlotte went alone to Roe Head at the age of fifteen and was separated from her siblings that she made lasting friendships with the Taylor sisters and with Ellen Nussey. It is significant that Emily and Anne seem to have made no important friendships throughout their lives. Emily, of course, spent less time away from home than any of the others, and presumably Anne, working as a governess, had limited opportunities for forming and developing relationships. In any case, their closeness to each other must have made other friendships less necessary to them.

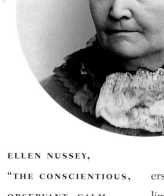

ELLEN NUSSEY,
"THE CONSCIENTIOUS,
OBSERVANT, CALM,
WELL-BRED
YORKSHIRE GIRL".

ELLEN NUSSEY

Of the friends Charlotte made at school, the most important both for her and for us is Ellen Nussey. Charlotte's correspondence with Ellen is the invaluable source of much of the contemporary information we have about the Brontës' lives and about Charlotte's thoughts and opinions. It was Ellen, too, who provided Mrs Gaskell with a lot of material for her biography of Charlotte. Arthur Bell Nicholls – who considered Charlotte's letters "dangerous as Lucifer matches" – exacted a promise from Ellen to destroy all Charlotte's correspondence. Fortunately for us, Ellen – who did not like Nicholls – did not keep that promise. Had she done so, the loss to Brontë scholarship would have been enormous.

It is chiefly to this correspondence with Ellen that we owe the insight we have into Charlotte's life at the Parsonage. In one letter, written early in their friendship, she describes how each day is the same as any other – teaching her sisters and drawing all morning, then walking till dinner, sewing till teatime and spending the evening reading, writing, doing "a little fancy work" or drawing again. Seven years later, just before Branwell's departure for Broughton in Furness, she speaks of "our plain monotonous mode of life" and how they are " as busy as possible … shirt-making and collar-stitching". Charlotte's dependence on Ellen's friendship is clear in a letter she wrote to her in July 1836, when Ellen was planning a visit to Haworth:

Every day during the last fortnight I have been expecting to hear from you, but seeing that no intelligence arrives I begin to get a little anxious. When will you come?

And, in September of the same year, she concluded another letter to Ellen with:

I wish I could live with you always, I begin to cling to you more fondly than ever I did. If we had but a cottage and a competency of our own I do think we might live and love on till <u>Death</u> without being dependent on any third person for happiness.

There is no doubt that, however close Charlotte felt to her sisters, she had a real need for intimate friendships with other women outside her own family. Ellen fulfilled that need, as did Mary Taylor, to a lesser extent. Of her friendship with Ellen – by that time all the more important to her since she had lost her sisters – Charlotte was to write later to William Smith Williams: "…affection was first a germ, then a sapling – then a strong tree: now, no friend … could be to me what Ellen is, yet she is no more than a conscientious, observant, calm, well-bred Yorkshire girl."

MARY TAYLOR

Charlotte's friendship with Mary Taylor was of a different kind. If Ellen provided her with the calm, stable, consistent support which Charlotte needed, Mary brought to her relationship with Charlotte a more adventurous, exciting spirit. She was a strikingly independent young woman, determined to make her own way in the world, which she did with great success. Like Charlotte and Emily, she and her sister Martha spent some time at school in Brussels – Martha died of cholera there – and she went on to teach in Germany. She then decided to join her brother in New Zealand, where she helped him to run a general store. She later published a series of articles and a novel, *Miss Miles: A Tale of Yorkshire Life Sixty Years Ago*, both of which were concerned with the struggle of women against the conventional limitations imposed on them.

ELIZABETH GASKELL

Charlotte's friendship with Elizabeth Gaskell, whom she met in 1850 when they were both well known for their respective novels *Jane Eyre* and *Mary Barton*, was significant and fortuitous. Having lost both Emily and Anne, Charlotte found in Mrs Gaskell a friend whose kindness and concern for her well-being were comforting and sustaining. Charlotte's response to an invitation to stay with the Gaskells shows just how much she needed such a friend at this stage in her life:

> *If anybody would tempt me from home you would … the feeling expressed in your letter … goes <u>right home</u> where you would have it go, and heals as you would have it to heal.*

After Charlotte's death, when gossip and rumour about her life began to circulate in the press, it was to Mrs Gaskell that Patrick – encouraged by Ellen – turned in his search for an "official" biographer of his famous daughter.

BRANWELL'S FRIENDSHIPS

There is no evidence that Branwell, although he did have some friends, enjoyed the intimacy with any of them which Charlotte did with hers. Indeed, there is every indication that he did not, as his letter to Francis Grundy in 1846 suggests:

> *If I could see you it would be a sincere pleasure, but … Perhaps your memory of me may be dimmed, for you have known little in me worth remembering; but I still think often with pleasure of yourself, though so different from me in head and mind.*

Branwell first met Francis Grundy, a young engineer for the railways, while he was working at Luddenden Foot station. He and the sculptor, Joseph Leyland, encouraged Branwell to write, with some success, for it was at this time that he published his first poem in the *Halifax Guardian*. Perhaps Branwell's most constant friend over the years was John Brown, the sexton of Haworth Church. They were drinking companions and correspondents, and it was to him that Branwell's last pathetic letter was written, asking John Brown to get him "Five pence worth of Gin."

MARY TAYLOR, CHARLOTTE'S INDEPENDENT, ADVENTUROUS FRIEND FROM ROE HEAD DAYS.

FRIENDS AND COMPANIONS

ROMANCES

WILLIAM WEIGHTMAN, THE CURATE WHO "SAT OPPOSITE TO ANNE AT CHURCH SIGHING SOFTLY".

THE BRONTËS WERE NOT lucky in love. None of the children – except Charlotte very briefly – grew up to make the stable, fulfilling relationship that Patrick enjoyed with Maria until her death.

If Emily ever formed a romantic attachment, we know nothing of it. There has been much speculation, of course, about the writer of *Wuthering Heights*. How could she have created the passionate relationship between Cathy

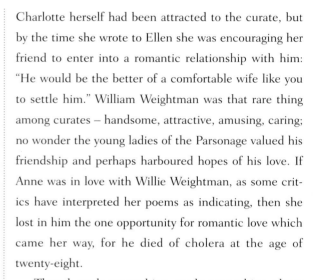

and Heathcliff if she had never experienced such a relationship herself? We are not going to try to answer that question here; but it is worth remembering that the Brontë children were reared on romantic fiction and poetry: and their imaginations were engaged in the intensity of such works, and in the emotions of their characters.

Brontë biographers are divided on whether or not Anne loved her father's curate, William Weightman. Angeline Goreau claims that "He was very probably the love of her life". Certainly, Charlotte wrote to Ellen Nussey describing how he,

… sits opposite to Anne at Church sighing softly – & looking out of the corners of his eyes to win her attention – & Anne is so quiet, her look so downcast – they are a picture.

Charlotte herself had been attracted to the curate, but by the time she wrote to Ellen she was encouraging her friend to enter into a romantic relationship with him: "He would be the better of a comfortable wife like you to settle him." William Weightman was that rare thing among curates – handsome, attractive, amusing, caring; no wonder the young ladies of the Parsonage valued his friendship and perhaps harboured hopes of his love. If Anne was in love with Willie Weightman, as some critics have interpreted her poems as indicating, then she lost in him the one opportunity for romantic love which came her way, for he died of cholera at the age of twenty-eight.

Though we know nothing, or almost nothing, about any romantic attachments of the two younger sisters, we know a lot about Branwell's and Charlotte's passionate affairs. As we've seen, the great romantic passion of Charlotte's life was for her Brussels teacher, Monsieur Heger. That her love was unrequited by the apparently happily married man only added to her anguish. On her return to Haworth, such was her distress that she poured out in several letters to him her suffering and sense of loss:

I will tell you candidly that during this time of waiting I have tried to forget you, for the memory of a person one believes one is never to see again, and whom one nevertheless greatly respects, torments the mind exceedingly and when one has suffered this kind of anxiety for one or two years, one is ready to do anything to regain peace of mind. I have done everything; I have sought occupations, I have absolutely forbidden myself the pleasure of speaking about you – even to Emily …

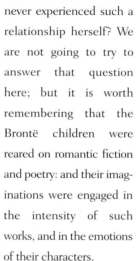

and she goes on to describe herself as "the slave of a dominant and fixed idea which has become a tyrant over one's mind".

It is not difficult to see here the passionate longing for a reciprocated romantic love which bears fruit in *Jane Eyre* and *Villette*. It is not surprising that Charlotte took so long to accept Arthur Bell Nicholls' proposal of marriage: what he offered was a steady, stable love of quite a different kind from the one she had grown up to expect and want. Like the Irish poet Yeats, she had suffered all the pangs of rejected romantic love before finding, in marriage, "a glad kindness" which brought her brief but profound happiness.

BRANWELL'S LOVES

Branwell was not so fortunate. As a man, his opportunities for romantic attachments were much greater than his sisters', and it appears he took advantage of them, though the only really serious affair was towards the end of his life, with his employer's wife, Mrs Robinson. As we've already mentioned, a recent source, according to Juliet Barker, suggests that Branwell had a passing sexual affair with a young woman, probably one of the servants, while he was tutor to the Postlethwaite boys at Broughton in Furness, and that there was a daughter born of this union. If this was so, there's no evidence to suggest the affair made a lasting or profound impression on Branwell.

The effect of his relationship with Mrs Robinson, however, was disastrous. Dismissed from his post at Thorp Green, he was inconsolable. Like Charlotte, he had fallen in love with somebody already married, and like her he was devastated by the loss. Unlike her, though, he told his story to everyone who would listen, pouring out his despair and grief with a lack of self-control which horrified his family. In a letter to Francis Grundy in 1845 he wrote: "I have lain during nine long weeks utterly shattered in body and broken down in mind … Eleven continuous nights of sleepless horror reduced me to almost blindness". He concluded by "Apologising sincerely for what seems like whining egotism". When Lydia Robinson's husband died in 1846 and

Branwell expected her to summon him to her side, he was doubly devastated by a message sent by her coachman indicating that he must not on any account see her or she would be disinherited under the terms of her husband's will. In fact, there was no such clause in the will, and Lydia Robinson went on to marry a rich relative just weeks after Branwell's death.

For Charlotte particularly, the public spectacle of Branwell's grief must have been hard to witness. Her lack of sympathy for him during the last few years of his life was not just for the wasted talent, surely, but because he had not the moral fibre and self-control to bear the same affliction as she suffered in silence.

THE OBJECT OF CHARLOTTE'S PASSION, M. HEGER, AND HIS FAMILY.

"DESOLATION AND BITTERNESS"

WHO WERE THE BRONTËS ?

A FEW DAYS after Anne's funeral Charlotte wrote to Smith Williams, describing her reaction to Anne's – and Emily's – death, and her sense of loss and loneliness:

Her quiet, Christian death did not rend my heart as Emily's stern, simple, undemonstrative end did. I let Anne go to God, and felt He had a right to her. I could hardly let Emily go. I wanted to hold her back then, and I want her back now. Anne, from her childhood, seemed preparing for an early death. Emily's spirit seemed strong enough to bear her to fulness of years. They are both gone, and so is poor Branwell, and Papa has now me only – the weakest, puniest, least promising of his six children. Consumption has taken the whole five.

Charlotte had lost not only her siblings; she had lost, too, her fellow writers, those with whom she had shared her whole creative apprenticeship and maturity. She and Branwell had created their early stories together; the sisters had sat together writing at the dining room table and walked round it reading the manuscripts of their novels out loud to each other. Together they had faced the world. Her words better than any others convey what it felt like to return alone to the house they had shared:

I got home a little before eight o'clock. All was clean and bright waiting for me – Papa and the servants were well – and all received me with an affection which should have consoled. The dogs seemed in strange ecstasy. I am certain they regarded me as the harbinger of others – the dumb creatures thought that as I was returned – those who had been so long absent were not far behind.

THE FORMAL TRAPPINGS OF DEATH IN VICTORIAN ENGLAND.

I left Papa soon and went into the dining-room – I shut the door – I tried to be glad that I was come home… I felt that the house was all silent – the rooms were all empty. I remembered where the three were laid – in what narrow dark dwellings – never were they to reappear on earth. So the sense of desolation and bitterness took possession of me – the agony that <u>was to be undergone</u>, and <u>was not</u> to be avoided came on.

And to Mr Williams she wrote: "waking I think – sleeping I dream of them". To him, also, she spoke of the rebellious rage she felt and how "my heart revolts against the burden of solitude". The days, she said, were not so bad because she was occupied with household tasks and responsibilities; but to Ellen Nussey she confessed: "The great trial is when evening closes and night approaches – At that hour we used to assemble in the dining-room – we used to talk – Now I sit by myself – necessarily I am silent," Anne's heroine, Agnes Grey , thinking about her father's death, says,

We often pity the poor, because they have no leisure to mourn their departed relatives, and necessity obliges them to labour through their severest afflictions; but is not active employment the best remedy for overwhelming sorrow … the surest antidote for despair? It may be a rough comforter: it may seem hard to be harrassed with the cares of life when we have no relish for its enjoyments … but is not labour better than the rest we covet? and are not those petty, tormenting cares less hurtful than a continual brooding over the great affliction that oppresses us?

Charlotte knowing that there was, indeed, only one answer to her loss, echoes Agnes Grey. She wrote to Smith Williams, "Labour must be the cure, not sympathy – labour is the only radical cure for rooted sorrow." With great difficulty and, no doubt, great self-discipline, she returned to the writing of *Shirley* and absorbed herself in that task all through the summer following Anne's death. She said of it, "writing it has been a boon to me – it took me out of dark and desolate reality to an unreal but happier region." Mrs Gaskell writes of Charlotte's "continual feeling of ill-health" following the completion of *Shirley*. It was to be a recurring pattern, and a cause for concern to both her father and Charlotte.

With time, of course, Charlotte learned to deal with her loss, as she had to. There is no doubt that her religious faith, and her strong belief in a life beyond this one, comforted and supported her. Emily and Anne, like the rest of her family, had gone to a better world.

The years that followed saw the writing and publication of *Villette* and Charlotte's acceptance into the established literary world. The loss of her sisters and overwhelming loneliness forced Charlotte to look beyond the Parsonage for companionship and emotional support. These she found, in some measure at least, with old friends and new ones, and certainly in her brief, happy and fulfilling marriage to Arthur Bell Nicholls.

PORTRAIT OF CHARLOTTE BY GEORGE RICHMOND, A WELL-KNOWN PORTRAIT ARTIST OF CHARLOTTE'S DAY.

"DESOLATION AND BITTERNESS"

CHARLOTTE'S MARRIAGE

Of late years, an abundant shower of curates has fallen upon the north of England: they lie very thick on the hills; every parish has one or more of them; they are young enough to be very active, and ought to be doing a great deal of good.

PHOTOGRAPH OF ARTHUR BELL NICHOLLS, PATRICK'S CURATE AND CHARLOTTE'S HUSBAND.

CHARLOTTE'S NOVEL *Shirley* opens with an ironic attack on three curates, including one from Ireland. That she had had considerable experience of observing clerical comportment among her father's curates is clear from the portraits she paints of Donne, Sweeting and Malone. It is clear, too, that she had not formed a very high opinion of them or their worth, although there was one among the Haworth curates, William Weightman, whom all the Brontë family liked and respected. His death from cholera in 1842 was a source of great grief to both them and the whole community.

Weightman was, however, the exception; and when Arthur Bell Nicholls arrived in Haworth to work as Patrick's curate in 1845, nobody – least of all Charlotte – would have foreseen that he was to become her husband. Indeed, Charlotte was still writing passionate letters to Monsieur Heger at the time, and her comments on Mr Nicholls are hardly encouraging: "his narrowness of mind always strikes me chiefly," she wrote to Ellen Nussey and, when he had gone home to Ireland on holiday, "I am sorry to say that many of the parishioners express a desire that he should not trouble himself to re-cross the channel but should remain quietly where he is."

The creator of the juvenilia and Mr Rochester was not likely to find in Mr Nicholls the romantic partner who would replace in her affections the unattainable Monsieur Heger. Indeed, one suspects she would never have countenanced Nicholls' attentions had she not been so lonely after the death of Anne. That she did finally begin to notice him and respond to his affection aroused Patrick's fierce opposition – opposition which was overcome only with time and reluctance.

Patrick was afraid, it seems, that, were Charlotte to marry, her inevitable pregnancy would pose dangers for a woman of thirty-eight in delicate health. Aside from

known such comparative immunity from headache, sickness and indigestion", she wrote to Miss Wooler.

That marriage brought her comfort, companionship, security and fulfilment there is no doubt. Charlotte wrote to Ellen not long before she died:

I want to give you an assurance, which I know will comfort you – and that is, that I find in my husband the tenderest nurse, the kindest support, the best earthly comfort that ever woman had. His patience never fails, and it is tried by sad days and broken nights.

Mrs Gaskell records how, just before Charlotte's death,

Wakening for an instant from this stupor of intelligence, she saw her husband's woe-worn face, and caught the sounds of some murmured words of prayer that God would spare her. 'Oh!' she whispered forth, 'I am not going to die, am I? He will not separate us, we have been so happy.'

the fear of losing the last of his children, he also deemed Arthur Bell Nicholls not worthy of his now famous daughter. He did not attend the wedding, excusing himself on the grounds of ill-health. He was, of course, right to fear the physical consequences of her marrying. Within a few months of returning from their honeymoon in Ireland, Charlotte began to suffer a general deterioration in her health and violent bouts of nausea. In January 1855 it was clear that she was pregnant, and two months later she was dead. She had enjoyed just nine months of marriage.

They must have been nine months of considerable adjustment for Charlotte, who in the last few years had known financial independence and great literary acclaim. "[I]t is a solemn and strange and perilous thing for a woman to become a wife," she wrote to Ellen Nussey, with no further explanation of just why it was so. But there were very positive comments, too: "I think it [marriage] tends to draw you out of, and away from yourself". She speaks of Mr Nicholls' "protection which does not interfere" during her honeymoon in Ireland when he respected her wish to enjoy and respond alone and uninterrupted to the natural beauty around her.

Just as unhappiness had so often brought Charlotte ill-health, so, ironically, until she became pregnant, her health improved dramatically: "it is long since I have

CHARLOTTE'S
HONEYMOON DRESS,
WHICH, THOUGH
FADED, IS JUST
AS IT WAS WHEN
CHARLOTTE WORE IT.
ALL CONTEMPORARY
DESCRIPTIONS
OF CHARLOTTE
EMPHASIZE HER
SMALL STATURE,
WHICH THIS
DRESS CONFIRMS.

2 THE WORK OF THE BRONTËS

THE SHEER LITERARY OUTPUT of the Brontës is astonishing considering their short lives and that, for most of their adult years, they also had to earn a living. Charlotte wrote more than her sisters, of course: not only did she live longer, but her fame brought her the means to write full-time. Between them, the four surviving Brontë children created an impressive number of plays, stories and poems – the juvenilia produced in their years together at the Parsonage – nor was their creativity limited to writing: as any visitor to the Parsonage knows, they were constantly drawing and painting.

The first volume of work published by the Brontës was the 1846 collection of poems by the three sisters. As they grew into adulthood, their poetry combined their Angrian and Gondal worlds with a more personal voice, although it is often difficult to distinguish between the two, particularly in the case of Emily and Anne. Perhaps their natural reticence made it easier for them to speak through their Gondal characters. The lyric poem, after all, has the most personal of voices.

In addition to their juvenilia, poetry, novels and art, we have access to the Brontës' lives and minds through letters and "diary papers", a series of short exchanges between Emily and Anne. They were written, sometimes together, as diary entries to be opened at a future date, and give a vivid and immediate picture of the sisters' lives and their hopes for the future.

Of the novels, four are Charlotte's, two Anne's and one Emily's. A publishers' letter suggests that Emily may have been writing a second novel when she died; if so,

there is no trace of it. It is a source of both frustration and, perhaps, relief that there was no sequel to *Wuthering Heights*. Could she have equalled or surpassed the passionate intensity, the visual power, the compelling force of her first novel? Would a second have been an inevitable disappointment?

Both *Wuthering Heights* and *Jane Eyre* have passed into the classic literature of the nineteenth century. As great love stories, exciting interest and emotional involvement, they have attracted a romantic audience which has responded to them as both novels and dramatizations on stage or film. They are read and studied all over the world and have been translated into many languages. *Jane Eyre* is more accessible than Charlotte's later novels, *Shirley* and *Villette*, although many readers and critics would say *Villette* is her greatest achievement.

Anne, the least known of the Brontë sisters, nevertheless produced a novel once described as "the most perfect prose narrative in English literature", and in *The Tenant of Wildfell Hall* she wrote a novel years ahead of its time. Its concern with the breakdown of marriage, with women's right to determine – within a strong moral framework – their own futures and that of their children, makes it likely it will attract more, rather than less, attention in the future.

If the Brontë sisters could have looked forward from the 1820s to their position in the history of English literature, they would no doubt have been amazed – not least, one imagines, because their names, rather than Branwell's, are among the chosen.

THE JUVENILIA

Papa bought Branwell some soldiers at Leeds when papa came home it was night and we where in Bed so next morning Branwell came to our Door with a Box of soldiers Emily and I jumped out of Bed and I snat[c]hed up one and exclaimed this is the Duke of Wellington it shall be mine!! ... when I said this ... Emily likewise took one and said it should be hers when Anne came down she took one also. Mine was the prettiest of the whole and perfect in every part Emilys was a Grave Looking fellow we called him Gravey Anne's was a queer little thing very much like herself. he was called waiting Boy Branwell chose Bonaparte.

ONE OF THE NUM-
BERS OF "THE YOUNG
MEN'S MAGAZINE",
MODELLED ON THE
BRONTË CHILDREN'S
FAVOURITE, "BLACK-
WOOD'S MAGAZINE".

IN THIS NOW WELL-KNOWN (and very badly punctuated) account Charlotte described the eventful day, June 5, 1826, when their father's gift of a box of soldiers to Branwell inspired the young Brontës to embark upon creating an imaginary world which they were to inhabit long after most children have abandoned their childhood fantasies. This imaginary world went through a number of different phases, as the children's games and stories reflected not only their fantasies, but their interests and preoccupations in the actual world they inhabited. At first the games were dominated by Branwell: they were, after all, his soldiers – the Young Men, as the children called them – and he could indulge his interest in matters military, with the help of his siblings, by carrying out the latest campaigns of Wellington's war with France, which everyone was reading about in the newspapers.

Gradually, as might be expected, his sisters – particularly Charlotte – exerted more of their influence on the games. In "The Play of the Islanders", each of the children took a real island – Arran, Guernsey, Wight and Man – and peopled it with their own heroes. The list of these heroes, including well-known writers, statesmen, doctors and the editors of *Blackwood's Magazine*, testifies to the extraordinary wide general knowledge and reading of the young Brontës.

It was on *Blackwood's*, the Tory magazine, that the young Brontës modelled their own early writings. Indeed, both Charlotte and Branwell compiled their own *Blackwood's Young Men's Magazine*. In Glass Town there were newspapers, like "The Young Men's Intelligencer", suggested, no doubt, by those familiar to the Brontë household. In the tiny books which the children made and filled with minute handwriting, formed to look like real print, they created whole societies, peopled by men and women who fell in love, fought battles, felt jealousy and knew both suffering and happiness. The Brontë children became passionately involved in their lives.

When they took the Young Men to Ashantee, creating the Glass Town Confederacy, and, later, Angria, they showed a knowledge of the African continent probably gleaned from *Blackwood's* and old geography books. *A Grammar of General Geography*, at the Brontë Parsonage Museum, complete with the children's notes and drawings, confirms their familiarity with the real west Africa to which they transported the Twelves – as the Young Men were now called. True children of their time, the Brontës were clearly interested in the colonial world and they responded imaginatively to it.

Besides their reading of *Blackwood's* and their knowledge of history and geography, there were other sources that fed their hungry imaginations: the *Arabian Nights* no doubt inspired them to create their own Chief Genii, the protectors of the Twelves in Ashantee, and Byron and Scott in particular furnished them with an awareness and understanding of many kinds of events and relationships which they created in their early writing. Public figures, too, found their way into the stories, most notably Wellington, Charlotte's hero from the first moment she saw the soldiers, and his eldest son, the Marquis of Douro, who, as Zamorna, became King of Angria. For many years, Branwell and Charlotte, the eldest of the children, were the dominant creators of the little books, peopling them with their heroes and heroines – often showing considerable rivalry over determining the plot and the fate of their characters. In 1831, however, Emily and Anne formed their own kingdom, Gondal; they were to continue to move in and out of this world long after they became young women. As Branwell was, at least at the start, the most dominant creator of Angria, Emily was the most passionate force behind Gondal. Unfortunately, none of the prose stories of Gondal have survived, but many of Emily's best poems were part of its saga.

In both Angria and Gondal are to be found, of course, characters who prepare us for Jane Eyre and Rochester,

Heathcliff and Catherine Earnshaw. Fanny Ratchford refers nicely to aspects of the novels that "come from the days of the wooden soldiers". In the juvenilia, after all, the young Brontës were serving their apprenticeship as novelists. Their mature works were born, not suddenly and without preparation, but as a result of an imaginative and creative process which began years before.

It is difficult to read or think about these early writings without being conscious of the very important part Branwell played in their creation and, therefore, in the development of his sisters' genius. There was nothing to suggest, as they were all growing up and writing together, that Branwell alone would be the one who did not fulfil the literary promise of his youth.

LITERARY INFLUENCES

ALL THE BRONTË CHILDREN read voraciously whatever they could lay their hands on. Their father's books were available to them; it is possible they had access to the library at nearby Ponden Hall, the home of the Heaton family; and it is probable that they borrowed from the Keighley circulating libraries. There they would have found a wide variety of books and periodicals on the kinds of subjects likely to feed their young imaginations: history, travel, biography, fiction, poetry.

By far the most important periodical for the Brontë children was *Blackwood's Magazine*. Founded in 1817, it grew up with them and, as Juliet Barker says, it "formed the tastes and fed the interests of the Brontës for many years. They absorbed its Tory politics, made its heroes, from the Duke of Wellington to Lord Byron, into their own heroes and copied its serio-comic style."

It was in imitation of *Blackwood's* that the children produced *The Young Men's Magazine* in which they printed the Angrian chronicle, and from *Blackwood's* that they got the setting for Angria, inspired, no doubt, by the current interest in the exploration of Africa. It is not surprising that Branwell particularly aspired to contributing to the magazine which had so greatly influenced his own literary development.

SCOTT AND BYRON

Born at the end of the Romantic period, the Brontës were, nevertheless, essentially children of it. The great figures of the Romantic movement were their literary heroes and exemplars. In their preoccupation with the world of nature, with freedom, with the expression of emotion and the fulfilment of the individual, the Brontës were the natural offspring of Scott and Byron, the two writers who influenced them most strongly. In Scott they found the art of storytelling and passionate, romantic landscape, peopled by strong, adventurous characters. Like themselves and, as George Sampson comments, "Unlike Jane Austen, Scott was unnatural with the conventional and at ease with the eccentric."

ILLUSTRATION FROM WALTER SCOTT'S NOVEL "HEART OF MIDLOTHIAN".

They shared with him, as with Byron, an interest in the mysterious, the supernatural, the gothic. Charlotte was to write to Ellen, "For Fiction – read Scott alone all novels after his are worthless."

In the same letter, in which she is advising Ellen on what books to read, Charlotte tells her:

> *If you like poetry let it be first rate, Milton, Shakespeare,*
> *Thomson, Goldsmith Pope (if you will though I don't*
> *admire him) Scott, Byron, Camp[b]ell, Wordsworth and*
> *Southey Now Ellen don't be startled at the names of*
> *Shakespeare, and Byron. Both these were great Men and*
> *their works are like themselves, You will know how to*
> *chuse the good and avoid the evil, the finest passages are*
> *always the purest …*

Thus speaks the moral Victorian Charlotte to her "conscientious, observant, calm, well-bred Yorkshire girl." As Juliet Barker says, "One wonders, by contrast, what she might have suggested Mary Taylor should read."

THE SHADOW OF BYRON

In Charlotte's and Emily's novels, the shadow of Byron is most apparent in their heroes: they are outcast men, who destroy what they most love, and who are possessed by dark and demonic forces. Nevertheless, they fascinate and attract. Both Rochester and Heathcliff – and Arthur Huntingdon to some extent – share these characteristics.

Charlotte's and Emily's heroines, too, like Byron's heroes, are obsessed by love, as Harriet Martineau noted when reviewing *Villette*. Cathy brings the same destructive forces to their relationship as does Heathcliff, who says "savagely" to her when they meet for the last time:

> *Are you possessed with a devil … to talk in that manner*
> *to me, when you are dying?*

There were other influences, of course, on the Brontës. The Bible was one of these, and Wordsworth, a formative and profound influence on Patrick, and

undoubtedly through him on his children. So was William Cowper, the poet whom Anne specially loved and sympathized with. His love of animals would, no doubt, have attracted her to him; and his doubts about his own salvation and his extreme, suicidal melancholy were aspects of his character to which she could relate, as the poem she wrote to him suggests.

There is one poet whose advice, if not his influence, Charlotte resisted. In December 1836, when Charlotte was twenty, she wrote to Robert Southey, the poet laureate, asking his opinion of her poetry. His reply came in March 1837. In whatever world he now inhabits, it is tempting to think that Southey must still be regretting the advice he sent Charlotte:

> *Literature cannot be the business of a woman's life: & it*
> *ought not to be. The more she is engaged in her proper*
> *duties, the less leisure will she have for it, even as an*
> *accomplishment & a recreation.*

THE POEMS

One day, in the autumn of 1845, I accidentally lighted on a MS. volume of verse in my sister Emily's handwriting. Of course, I was not surprised, knowing that she could and did write verse: I looked it over, and something more than surprise seized me, – a deep conviction that these were not common effusions, nor at all like the poetry women generally write. I thought them condensed and terse, vigorous and genuine. To my ear, they had also a peculiar music – wild, melancholy, and elevating.

O WROTE CHARLOTTE in her "Biographical Notice of Ellis and Acton Bell", written to accompany the 1850 edition of *Wuthering Heights* and *Agnes Grey*. Charlotte went on to say:

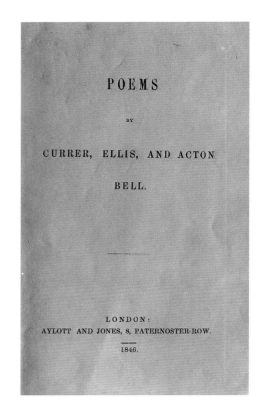

POEMS

BY

CURRER, ELLIS, AND ACTON

BELL.

LONDON:
AYLOTT AND JONES, 8, PATERNOSTER-ROW.

1846.

FRONTISPIECE OF THE FIRST EDITION OF THE "POEMS OF CURRER, ELLIS, AND ACTON BELL", 1846.

My sister Emily was not a person of demonstrative character, nor one, on the recesses of whose mind and feelings, even those nearest and dearest to her could, with impunity, intrude unlicensed; it took hours to reconcile her to the discovery I had made, and days to persuade her that such poems merited publication. I knew, however, that a mind like hers could not be without some latent spark of honourable ambition, and refused to be discouraged in my attempts to fan that spark to flame.

For Emily, the discovery of her poems was clearly both very upsetting and enraging. Many of the verses Charlotte read were Gondal poems, part of the secret world she shared with Anne – that her older sister should stumble into that world and insist that the poems be made public were intrusions that were very difficult for Emily to come to terms with.

Nor were Charlotte's motives purely altruistic. Having discovered Emily's verse, Charlotte then learned from Anne that she too had written verses, and, on reading them, thought they also "had a sweet sincere pathos of their own." Her "unlicensed" intrusion on Emily's privacy persuaded her that there was material available for a slim volume of poetry by all three sisters, and in May 1846 *Poems by Currer, Ellis and Acton Bell* was published, at the sisters' own expense. Charlotte explained their choice of names in the 1850 "Biographical Notice":

Averse to personal publicity, we veiled our own names under those of Currer, Ellis, and Acton Bell; the ambiguous choice being dictated by a sort of conscientious

scruple at assuming Christian names positively mascu-
line, while we did not like to declare ourselves women,
because … we had a vague impression that authoresses
are liable to be looked on with prejudice; we had noticed
how critics sometimes use for their chastisement the
weapon of personality, and for their reward, a flattery,
which is not true praise.

CONDENSED ENERGY

The poems and the pseudonyms that were to cause so
much curiosity the following year, when *Jane Eyre*,
Wuthering Heights and *Agnes Grey* were published,
passed almost, though not quite, without notice: "Who
are Currer, Ellis, and Acton Bell, we are nowhere
informed," wrote a reviewer in *The Critic*, who went on
to praise the poems effusively as possessing "more
genius than it was supposed this utilitarian age had
devoted to the loftier exercises of the intellect." One
critic, writing in the *Athenaeum*, recognized that Ellis'
poems might "yet find an audience in the outer world".
Nevertheless, only two copies of the book were sold in
the year following its publication: it did not look as if the
Bells were headed for fame.

It was left to Charlotte, who first discovered the
poems, to recognize that it was Emily's contribution that
would be of lasting literary merit:

I know no woman that ever lived ever wrote such poetry
before. Condensed energy, clearness, finish – strange,
strong pathos are their characteristics; utterly different
from the weak diffusiveness, the laboured yet most feeble
wordiness, which dilute the writings of even very popular
poetesses.

In contrast, she saw her own contribution to the 1846
volume as "chiefly juvenile productions", which "now
appear to me very crude." Many of Anne's poems are
religious in theme and reflect both the strong influence
of William Cowper and her own tendency towards
melancholy, whether the poems are personal or part of
the Gondal saga. Barbara and Gareth Lloyd Evans

describe them as possessing "a cool and lyrical reflec-
tiveness".

We have only to look at Emily's selection to see at
once that her poems are of a different order from her
sisters'. In the best of them we find the same kind of
power and sustained use of elemental imagery that are
to be found in *Wuthering Heights*.

Cold in the earth, and fifteen wild Decembers
From those brown hills, have melted into spring …

It is not just in the imagery that we see the likeness to
her novel. While Heathcliff managed his grief less con-
structively than the speaker of the poem, the lines of the
fifth stanza could be his:

No later light has lightened up my heaven,
No second morn has ever shone for me;
All my life's bliss from thy dear life was given –
All my life's bliss is in the grave with thee.

MANUSCRIPT OF
ONE OF EMILY'S
POEMS, DATED
MAY 28TH, 1838.

JANE EYRE

... highest moral offence a novel writer can commit, that of making an unworthy character interesting in the eyes of the reader. Mr Rochester is a man who deliberately and secretly seeks to violate the laws both of God and man, and yet we will be bound half our lady readers are enchanted with him for a model of generosity and honour. We would have thought that such a hero had had no chance, in the purer taste of the present day.

How wrong the reviewer was in this last sentence; how right that Rochester, the dark, Byronic hero, enchanted readers in Charlotte's own day, and continues to do so today.

ENCHANTMENT

But the hostile reviews were in the minority. Thackeray, the contemporary novelist whom Charlotte most admired, wrote to her publisher, who had sent him a copy of the novel, published under the pseudonym of Currer Bell. He writes, "I have been exceedingly moved and pleased by *Jane Eyre*. It is a woman's writing, but whose? Give my respects and thanks to the author, whose novel is the first English one ... I've been able to read for many a day ...". G.H. Lewes wrote in his review of December 1847:

... man or woman, young or old, be that as it may, no such book has gladdened our eyes for a long while. Almost all that we require in a novelist she has: perception of character, and power of delineating it; picturesqueness; passion; and knowledge of life. The story is not only of singular interest, naturally evolved, unflagging to the last, but it fastens itself upon your attention, and will not leave you. The book closed, the enchantment continues ...

YOUNG JANE LOCKED IN THE RED ROOM, AS PLAYED BY ANNA PAQUIN IN THE 1996 CINEMA VERSION OF THE BOOK.

CHARLOTTE BRONTË'S MASTERPIECE, *Jane Eyre*, hit the London literary scene with a bang when it was published on October 16, 1847. It was not without its critics, chiefly on the grounds of its improbability of plot, incident and character, its "coarseness" and its questionable moral and religious tone and attitude. Such criticisms, particularly the latter two, come as something of a surprise to the modern reader who almost certainly sees Jane's most important choices in life as profoundly moral and religious in nature.

It is difficult to transport ourselves back into a moral climate that could blame Charlotte Brontë for committing the:

And the enchantment has continued. *Jane Eyre* is the story of a young orphan girl, cruelly treated by her guardian, who is sent off to boarding-school, where she continues to suffer. She is then employed as a governess and falls in love with the master of the house – a recipe for disaster or for great happiness, as every reader of romantic fiction knows.

What makes *Jane Eyre* more significant than the average romantic novel? Told in the first person, the story of Jane's life unfolds in chronological order. Through her eyes we see the world which she inhabits and experience the events which formed her character. A highly imaginative child, she conveys visually and passionately her thoughts and feelings, so that the reader is drawn into them, as if experiencing the same events and emotions. When she suffers imprisonment in the red room or loneliness and humiliation at Lowood, the harsh boarding-school to which she is sent, the reader follows her there, drawn by the intensity of the feeling, by the visual imagery which dominates the book, by the gripping nature of the storytelling. And when Jane goes as a governess to Thornfield Hall, Charlotte – steeped in the romantic and Gothic world of Byron and Scott – holds the reader in breathtaking suspense worthy of any mystery story.

A MORAL TALE

But the novel is more than this. Unlike *Wuthering Heights*, and in spite of the early hostile reviews, *Jane Eyre* is profoundly moral; it is concerned with Jane's per-

sonal development into a balanced, just, principled, self-disciplined, complete woman. Only such a woman deserves the happiness of love fulfilled. She has to learn to restrain the undisciplined, passionate nature that distinguishes her at the start of the novel. Jane's friend at Lowood, Helen Burns – based on Charlotte's lost sister Maria – plays a major role in this; it is Helen who warns her against "the indulgence of resentment" so that when Jane pours out her grievances to Miss Temple, the principal of the school, she "infused into the narrative far less of gall and wormwood than ordinary."

What she begins to learn at Lowood, Jane must continue to perfect in her life as an adult, just as Rochester, the "fettered" bird and "caged eagle", has to learn to make right and just choices if he is to enjoy the freedom of love.

And, above all, of course, it is a love story, written with all the passionate intensity of a woman who had not been able to enjoy the emotional and sexual fulfilment of union with the man she loved. When Charlotte began her last chapter with the now famous words, "Reader, I married him", her unrequited love for Monsieur Heger bore fruition in fiction as it could not in real life.

AGNES GREY

IT IS NOT SURPRISING THAT, published together with *Wuthering Heights*, *Agnes Grey* received so little attention from the critics. Those who did review it made such comments as, "it has nothing to call for special notice" and "It leaves no painful impression on the mind – some may think it leaves no impression at all." Yet George Moore called it "the most perfect prose narrative in English literature." This same contradiction in response to the novel continues today: *Agnes Grey* still bores some readers, while charming others.

The novel is, as we have already seen, about a governess' life. Agnes, speaking in the first person, tells her own story, compiled from "My diary". The daughter of "a clergyman of the north of England" – like Anne herself – Agnes wants to give financial help to her straitened family by becoming independent. It is interesting to note, incidentally, that her mother suggests to her sister that she might contribute to the family's means by "trying to dispose of [her water-colour drawings] to some liberal picture-dealer" and even to Agnes, "I dare say you will be able to produce something we shall all be proud to exhibit." Perhaps ideas for *The Tenant of Wildfell Hall* were already taking shape in Anne's mind.

It is as a governess, however, that Agnes decides to make her way in the world – against her parents' wishes. The novel covers the two posts she fills, the first with the Bloomfield family, the second with the Murrays. Both families treat her with the arrogance, superiority and lack of consideration that was the common lot of governesses. The Bloomfield children are indulged, undisciplined and ignorant; Agnes' task is to teach them, but without the support of the parents it is impossible to accomplish. What emerges as the novel unfolds is that her problems do not simply tax her strength and ingenuity; they become moral dilemmas.

On her arrival at Wellwood – ironically named? – Agnes meets her young charges, and "Master Tom", aged seven, insists on showing her his bird traps. When asked by Agnes why he wants to trap birds and what he does with them, he replies: "Sometimes I give them to the cat; sometimes I cut them in pieces with my penknife; but the next, I mean to roast alive." This is the prelude to the horrific scene in which he brings home a whole nest of baby birds, which he intends to torture, and Agnes – appalled at the thought and "urged by a sense of duty" – drops a large stone on the nest in order to spare "the callow nestlings" a lingering death. For this she is reprimanded by Mrs Bloomfield who tells her "the

"YOU ARE ALONE AGAIN MISS GREY."

creatures were all created for our convenience" and "a child's amusement is scarcely to be weighed against the welfare of a soulless brute."

Agnes, who had left at home "My dear little friend, the kitten", judges people's characters by their attitudes to animals. Mr Weston, the curate with whom she falls in love in the second half of the novel, not only rescues Snap from the rat-catcher; he also saves the old cottager Nancy's "gentle friend the cat" from Murray's gamekeeper. These scenes in the novel emphasize much more than Agnes' attitude to animals, of course; they bring home to the reader the problems of conscience she faces working for employers who do not share her moral values. We see the same kind of dilemma in her attitude to the poor and sick when she works for the Murray family.

Her responsibilities with the Murrays are with much older children, the two young ladies, Rosalie and Matilda. With them, she has to contend with the same lack of consideration and superiority as at the Bloomfields, as well as witness the fatuous and vain flirtations of Rosalie with every available man in the district, including Agnes' secret choice, Edward Weston.

THE LONELINESS OF AGNES

What impresses us most, perhaps, about the life of Agnes Grey as a governess is her loneliness. The novel is full of references to her being alone, physically, emotionally, socially: walking behind the family to and from church, ignored by her "superiors" in conversation, left alone for hours in the sitting-room at Ashby Park, watching "the slowly lengthening shadows from the window" that are suggestive of "my own world within". While Agnes herself knows it only too well – "it was my business to hear, and not to speak"; "like one deaf and dumb, who could neither speak nor be spoken to" – Mr Weston is the only other character to understand her position: "You are alone again, Miss Grey."

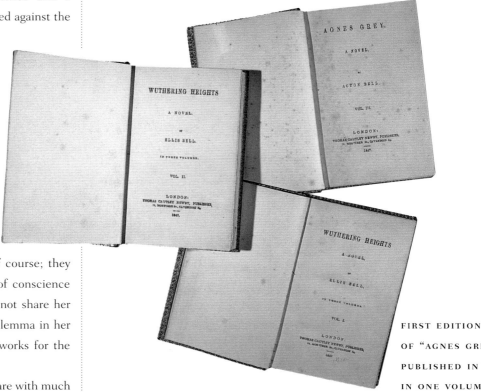

FIRST EDITION OF "AGNES GREY", PUBLISHED IN 1847 IN ONE VOLUME WITH EMILY'S "WUTHERING HEIGHTS".

Even this loneliness becomes a moral problem for her. At one point she contemplates "the joyless, hopeless, solitary path that lay before me" and says:

It was wrong to be so joyless, so desponding; I should have made God my friend, and to do His will the pleasure and the business of my life; but Faith was weak, and Passion was too strong.

Agnes' sense of duty, one is tempted to think, expresses Anne Brontë's own attitude and partially explains, perhaps, the "religious melancholy" into which she fell. Agnes – and one suspects Anne – blamed herself for not being contented with her lot in life, a lot which was, she believed, God-given.

Agnes Grey does leave the reader with the sense that the "passion" of which Agnes speaks is never fully explored or developed, and, when her mother says to her, "You always do things by extremes" we are rather surprised. The picture of Agnes this suggests is not the one we have seen – except in glimpses – throughout the novel.

WUTHERING HEIGHTS

"**W**UTHERING HEIGHTS was hewn in a wild workshop, with simple tools, out of homely materials" wrote Charlotte Brontë in her Preface to the 1850 edition of *Wuthering Heights*, published after Emily's death, "… her native hills were far more to her than a spectacle; they were what she lived in, and by, as much as the wild birds, their tenants, or as the heather, their produce".

Charlotte was in the uncomfortable position of trying to ensure that her sister's reputation would not rest alone on the hostile reviews that had greeted the publication of *Wuthering Heights*. She need not have worried, of course, that, as one critic put it, the book "will live a short and brilliant life, and then die and be forgotten"! *Wuthering Heights* had then and would continue to have its ardent admirers and devotees, those for whom the passionate power of the novel would make it strangely unique.

Emily chose to tell her story through several narrators. The novel opens with Lockwood, the first, arriving at Thrushcross Grange, the house he has rented from Heathcliff. It is his curiosity about his landlord and the household at Wuthering Heights that leads to Nelly, Lockwood's housekeeper, narrating the story that covers most of the novel. Within her narration, individual characters often tell their own stories in their own voices, usually through dialogue, but occasionally also in letters. It's a somewhat awkward structure, but the reader quickly becomes familiar with its design and purpose: the outsider narrator brings a different perspective on events and characters; the insider narrator has a knowledge and understanding important to the plot; the first-person voices of the characters enable them to speak as themselves, in their own language, and with their particular view of others and events.

POWER AND PASSION

What is it that makes *Wuthering Heights* so powerful? It's a novel dominated by the "native hills", of which Charlotte speaks, and by the passionate love of Heathcliff and Catherine for each other. It is their love, in all its elemental violence and cruelty, which is explored in the first half of the novel, and which continues to dominate till the end, as the loss of Catherine haunts and drives Heathcliff to his sadistic revenge and destruction.

Its power, of course, lies in the way that Emily Brontë has created her isolated, moorland world and developed her characters within it. When Mr Earnshaw

HEATHCLIFF AND CATHY AS PORTRAYED BY LAURENCE OLIVIER AND MERLE OBERON.

A DEMONIC HEATH-
CLIFF: "THE CLOUDED
WINDOWS OF HELL
FLASHED A MOMENT
TOWARDS ME." A
DESCRIPTION OF
HEATHCLIFF'S EYES
FROM CHAPTER 17
OF THE NOVEL.

arrives home bringing with him the young boy he has picked up in the streets of Liverpool – "starving, and houseless, and as good as dumb" – he introduces into the harmony of the Earnshaw family a discordant element that is going to have profound and unforeseen consequences at Wuthering Heights, the isolated farmhouse on the top of the moor. Hindley's broken fiddle, the present which his father had bought for him and had accidentally crushed on the way home while he was attending to Heathcliff, sets the scene symbolically for the destruction which Heathcliff is to wreak in the household.

As Heathcliff and Catherine grow closer, their relationship is expressed in the elemental images which dominate the novel: they are united not only in their common love of the moors but their souls are seen by Catherine as belonging to the same elemental forces, "… he's more myself than I am. Whatever our souls are made of, his and mine are the same, and Linton's is as different as a moonbeam from lightning, or frost from fire." And she goes on, " My love for Linton is like the foliage in the woods. Time will change it, I'm well aware, as winter changes the trees. My love for Heathcliff resembles the eternal rocks beneath – a source of little visible delight, but necessary – Nelly, I am Heathcliff."

Emily Brontë appeals to us through the language – the elemental images, lightning and fire, the eternal rocks, and through the rhythm of the prose; they are the vehicles in which she also presents us, of course, with a relationship between two people that most of her readers would like to experience themselves – not the violence, the betrayal, the sadistic revenge, but the union of soul and being which Catherine and Heathcliff see as the true nature of their love.

The second half of the novel, dominated by Heathcliff's loss and the relationships that develop between the younger generation of Earnshaws and Lintons, is often seen as much less powerful and interesting than the first half; but it is very important to the structure of *Wuthering Heights*, whether or not we see it as unravelling or resolving the conflicts of the novel. Its well-known ending, with its peaceful image of the moorland graves, is a fitting reminder that this is a complex novel.

Did Emily really intend the second half to resolve the conflicts of the first, as many critics have thought? What has happened to the ghosts walking the moor? As Lockwood – the outsider whose view of things is not wholly reliable – has the last word, the reader is left to decide for him or herself:

> *I lingered round them, under that benign sky; watched the moths fluttering among the heath and hare-bells; listened to the soft wind breathing through the grass; and wondered how any one could ever imagine unquiet slumbers for the sleepers in that quiet earth.*

THE TENANT OF WILDFELL HALL

tor, Gilbert Markham, writes a letter to his friend Halford, saying he will tell him "a tale of many chapters", "a return of confidence" for Halford's telling him about his early years. The story he goes on to tell is the story of his love for Helen Huntingdon, alias Graham. He recounts the story until the moment when Helen gives him her diary to read; from that moment – for most of the novel – she becomes the narrator through her diary. This simple flashback method is much less complicated than the structure of *Wuthering Heights*; the story is easy to follow and we are never confused between diary time and present time, as we sometimes are in Emily's novel.

We are introduced to Helen as a figure of scandal and gossip but, far from being a "loose" woman with low moral standards, she is, in fact, as devoted to duty and principle as is Jane Eyre. She leaves her husband because she fears for the moral welfare of their son, Arthur, and she returns to nurse her husband when he is dying, considering it her duty to support him. Although we sympathize with her torment and suffering at this point, she is unattractive in this role: her overt and articulate proselytizing smacks too much of the preacher – which her husband calls her – and of self-satisfaction.

Charlotte is much more sensitive than Anne when she presents Jane's conflict as between two abstractions

HELEN GRAHAM (TARA FITZGERALD) WITH GILBERT MARKHAM (TOBY STEPHENS), UNITED AT THE END OF THE NOVEL.

HELEN WITH HER SON ARTHUR.

A HEAD OF ITS TIME, *The Tenant of Wildfell Hall* is the story of a woman who leaves her alcoholic husband to protect herself and their son from his corruption. In a time when women of her class were expected to marry or stay at home with their fathers or, at the very boldest, become teachers and governesses, Helen Huntingdon earns her living by working as a painter.

The novel has a flashback–diary structure, not unlike that of *Wuthering Heights*. Its first-person narra-

– Principle and Passion. Jane has to make a moral choice over Rochester, but it is not laboured; and in *Jane Eyre* the presence of St John as an unattractive Christian character serves to distance both Jane and the novel from a direct Christian message of how to pursue the good. In contrast, Helen – despite her assurances that she believes in universal salvation and that Huntingdon has only to repent to be saved – smugly and constantly alludes to God, heaven and "the right way" in a manner that the modern reader finds difficult to accept without criticism and a sense of discomfort.

The story is absorbing and there is more humour in the novel than there is in either *Jane Eyre* or *Wuthering Heights*. There is also considerable irony, usually quite conscious. In this and in their emphasis on social niceties, awareness of class and the characters' preoccupation with marriage and money, the opening chapters are reminiscent of Jane Austen.

In contrast, however, Anne Brontë conveys anger, frustration, violence and resentment with a sureness that indicates she has experienced them. It is obvious that she has seen men drunk and is aware not only of the degradation and dissolution, but also of the cruelty and sadism that alcohol can bring with it. She has to convince us of its corrupting effects if we are to accept her need to leave Huntingdon to "save" Arthur and herself – since Huntingdon's corruption leaves *her* in moral danger, too, as the pursuit of Hargrave and Markham makes clear.

It is both ironic and tragic that Branwell, the gifted and promising brother of the juvenilia, should have provided his sisters with a model for the dissolute and drunken behaviour of both Hindley and Huntingdon.

If we were tempted to believe that the youngest Brontë was the quiet, gentle woman Charlotte paints for us, *The Tenant of Wildfell Hall* would surely force us to question our acceptance. In spite of the moral stance adopted in the novel, it is, in many ways, closer to the violent emotions of *Wuthering Heights* than to *Jane Eyre*.

In her introduction to the Penguin Classics edition of *The Tenant of Wildfell Hall*, Winifred Gérin reminds us that May Sinclair, an early Brontë biographer, wrote

HELEN MARRIES
THE DISSOLUTE
HUNTINGDON
(RUPERT GRAVES).

in 1913: "the slamming of Helen Huntingdon's bedroom door against her husband reverberated throughout Victorian Britain." Anne herself, aware of hostility to the subject of her novel – despite its popularity among readers – was to defend her position in the Preface to the second edition in characteristically moral terms:

> *I wished to tell the truth, for truth always conveys its own moral … Is it better to reveal the snares and pitfalls of life to the young and thoughtless traveller, or to cover them with branches and flowers? … if there were less of this delicate concealment of facts … there would be less of sin and misery to the young of both sexes who are left to wring their bitter knowledge from experience …*

It is interesting – but not surprising – to note that Charlotte, determined to safeguard Anne's reputation as the "gentle" sister, was never reconciled to *The Tenant*, saying of it:

> *The choice of subject was an entire mistake. Nothing less congruous with the writer's nature could be conceived.*

THE PROFESSOR
AND VILLETTE

CHARLOTTE'S FIRST NOVEL, *The Professor*, was published in June 1857, two years after her death and just over two months after the publication of Mrs Gaskell's *Life of Charlotte Brontë*. The timing was intentional: her husband, father, friends and publishers all feared a hostile reception to the novel. It was intended that Mrs Gaskell's biography make readers sympathetic to Charlotte's story and her treatment of it. In her own Preface, Charlotte spoke of the problems she had had trying to see the novel into print, commenting that "Men in business are usually thought to prefer the real", but her experience with *The Professor* was that it was too "real": "publishers … would have liked something more imaginative and poetical"; their preference was "for the wild, wonderful, and thrilling."

"Wild, wonderful, and thrilling" *The Professor* certainly wasn't; aware of this lack, Charlotte introduced into *Villette* incidents and aspects of character which can only be described as gothic, melodramatic or sensational. There is little of real suspense or mystery in *The Professor*; in *Villette* they abound.

Both novels are set in Brussels and were inspired by Charlotte's time there and her love for Monsieur Heger. As Emily and Anne seem to have been ambivalent about their male narrators in *Wuthering Heights* and *The Tenant of Wildfell Hall*, so perhaps was Charlotte about

AN ILLUSTRATION OF CRIMSWORTH HALL FROM "THE PROFESSOR".

William Crimsworth: whatever the reason, the male teacher–narrator of *The Professor* becomes the female teacher–narrator of *Villette*. Both, like Jane Eyre, are emotionally isolated characters.

William Crimsworth, the narrator and "hero" of *The Professor*, is orphaned and alone in the world when he goes to work for a cruel brother, a mill-owner, who only accentuates his loneliness by treating him like a "slave". On the advice of a Mr Hunsden, William decides to go to Brussels in search of work and independence, and there he becomes a teacher in a boys' school and subsequently at the nearby girls' school. While there he meets the young Swiss girl, Frances Evans Henri, to whom he gives English lessons. It is their relationship which develops in the second half of the novel.

The heroine of *Villette*, Lucy Snowe, also goes as a teacher to a Brussels school, where the "directrice", Madame Beck, is as unprincipled and dissembling as Mademoiselle Reuter of *The Professor*. Madame Beck plots and spies, "listening and peeping through a spyhole"; she is found "stealing like a cat", while Mademoiselle Reuter's glances were "not given in full, but out of the corners, so quietly, so stealthily", and she is described as "the crafty little politician".

Both novels present very similar pictures of Belgian school life: unintelligent girls, with no intellectual curiosity or interest, minds "subjected" by their Catholic faith, as Charlotte – with all her Protestant prejudice – declares in *The Professor*. Of one of the girls, Sylvie, who was destined for the cloister, she writes that she was "giving up her independence of thought and action into the hands of some despotic confessor." And she presents the priest in *Villette* as, hearing "unshocked" and absolving "unreluctant", confessions of lying: "it was the most venial of faults."

THEMES AND IMAGERY

What makes *The Professor* interesting to readers of Charlotte's other novels is this evidence of themes and imagery which she is going to develop in her later writing. The first part of *The Professor* is full of references to William's lack of and longing for liberty and independence: "I had the conviction that he could only regard me as a poor-spirited slave", William thinks as he passes Mr Hunsden's house; while working at his brother's factory, he records how "I sprang from my bed with other slaves", and to his brother he declares that his work is "the most nauseous slavery under the sun". Readers will remember that Jane Eyre sees John Reed as a "slave-driver" and herself as a "rebel slave" at Gateshead. Both seek escape from their positions through "independence" and "liberty": "I was a free, independent traveller," says William, having left his brother's slavery and before he gains employment in Brussels.

The thematic connections between all Charlotte's novels are fascinating and worth exploring. In *Villette* we find the same conflict between reason or principle and imagination or emotion as we find in *Jane Eyre*: the struggle to balance the two opposing sides of one's nature – "a vein of reason ever ran through her passion", comments Lucy admiringly of Miss Marchmont. And in both *Jane Eyre* and *Villette* houses and rooms take on a metaphorical, symbolic role, as they also do in *Wuthering Heights*.

In *The Professor* we find the embryonic *Villette*. The plot of the earlier novel is much simpler and much more realistic, and the characters less complex and less devel-

oped. In *Villette* the love of Lucy Snowe for her "professor", Paul Emmanuel, develops only in the last part of the novel; the first is dominated by her interest in Dr John and his infatuation with one of the empty-headed girls at the school before he settles his affections on a childhood friend. *Villette* is perhaps Charlotte's most interesting novel – some critics would say her greatest; *The Professor* sheds some interesting light on its conception and development.

A 1907 ILLUSTRA-
TION TO "VILLETTE".

SHIRLEY

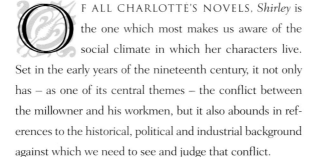

ILLUSTRATION BY
C.E. BROCK OF
SHIRLEY.

O F ALL CHARLOTTE'S NOVELS, *Shirley* is the one which most makes us aware of the social climate in which her characters live. Set in the early years of the nineteenth century, it not only has – as one of its central themes – the conflict between the millowner and his workmen, but it also abounds in references to the historical, political and industrial background against which we need to see and judge that conflict.

TROUBLED TIMES

Robert Moore, the millowner, with whom his cousin Caroline Helstone is very clearly in love at the start of the novel, is in dispute with his mill-workers because he is introducing into the mill machinery which threatens their jobs. Caroline's uncle praises his "hard spirit" and "resolution not 'to truckle with the mob'".

Moore is presented as a man in conflict with himself, forced by economic circumstances to be tougher, more ruthless than he would, by nature, be. Caroline accuses him of behaving at the mill "As if your living cloth-dressers were all machines like your frames and shears" and, when he reads *Coriolanus* aloud to her, of taking the side of "that proud patrician who does not sympathize with his famished fellow-men …". We see, though, in his treatment of the "noble" workman, William Farren, a sensitivity and concern that Moore considers he can ill afford in most of his dealings.

His many references to how the Orders in Council, prohibiting trade with America, are threatening him with financial ruin serve not only to enable us to see his point of view and sympathize with his position but also to place the events very firmly in their period. We learn that the French Revolution was responsible for the final ruin of the family business in Antwerp and that Mr Helstone reads in his morning newspaper "long despatches from General Lord Wellington: because "new movements had just taken place in the Peninsula".

From Mr Yorke, that robust, explosive, outspoken character whom Charlotte Brontë describes as "one of the most honourable and capable men in Yorkshire", we get an outburst on the state of the country:

What chance was there of reason being heard in a land that was king-ridden, priest-ridden, peer ridden – where a lunatic was the nominal monarch, an unprincipled debauchee the real ruler; where such an insult to common sense as hereditary legislators was tolerated … such an arrogant abuse as a pampered, persecuting established Church was endured and venerated …?

Nowhere else in Charlotte's fiction do we find the serious and repeated engagement in political dispute that we find in *Shirley*.

A PERSONAL EXPRESSION

But the novel is also a very personal expression of her own preoccupations and emotions. Started in 1848, the year which saw the deaths of both Branwell and Emily, it was finished in 1849 in the summer which followed Anne's death. As we've already said, Charlotte saw the writing of it as the only way of coping with her grief, and the evidence of that can be seen in various aspects of the novel. Shirley Keeldar, according to Mrs Gaskell, "is Charlotte's representation of Emily …. had she been placed in health and prosperity". To present to the world in a very positive way the sister who had been so misunderstood by it must have been a cathartic experience for Charlotte. "Captain Keeldar" Shirley likes to be called, reminding us of Monsieur Heger's comment about

Emily: "She should have been a man – a great navigator"; and we can hear Emily, with her love and trust of animals and her lack of "regard to any human creature", in Shirley's statement about whom she would consult on the nature of any man she loved:

Neither man nor woman, elderly nor young: – the little Irish beggar that comes barefoot to my door; the mouse that steals out of the cranny in the wainscot; the bird that in frost and snow pecks at my window for a crumb; the dog that licks my hand and sits beside my knee.

It isn't just in the fact that she chose to model Shirley on Emily, though, that we see the legacy of Charlotte's loss. Solitude and isolation were recurring themes in her novels, but Caroline is constantly presented as obsessed by the loneliness which faces her if Shirley and Moore marry, as she thinks they will:

She has him now: he is her lover; she is his darling … I do not grudge them their bliss; but I groan under my own misery …

Banned from Moore's house by her uncle, Caroline talks of his parlour as "her earthly paradise; how she longed to return to it, as much almost as the First Woman, in her exile, must have longed to revisit Eden." And when she quotes Cowper's *The Castaway* to Shirley, she is surely responding to as heartfelt an anguish – if differently inspired – as her own.

Not only had Charlotte lost all her siblings by the time she finished *Shirley*; she also knew all about the unrequited love which Caroline is tormented by: "A lover masculine so disappointed can speak and urge explanation; a lover feminine can say nothing."

The more complex nature of *Shirley* – combining, as it does, the personal fortunes of her characters with the socially, politically and historically realistic background and setting – marks the novel out from Charlotte's other fiction. It is not perhaps surprising that, with the exception of *The Professor*, it's probably the least well known of her novels.

AN 1872 ILLUSTRATION FROM "SHIRLEY", BY E.M. WIMPERIS.

REVIEWS OF THE NOVELS

ALMOST ALL of the Brontë novels, when they first appeared in print, were attacked by the critics for being "coarse", or for having a questionable moral and religious purpose. Both *Jane Eyre* and *Shirley* were also criticized for being "improbable" or "unreal".

The plot of *Jane Eyre* was greeted as "most extravagantly improbable, verging all along upon the supernatural, and at last running fairly into it", and another critic said of the novel:

> *I cannot understand why the author of Jane Eyre could not have found a simpler action through which to develop her situation and characters; I cannot understand why she should have thought she needed to have such complicated and disjointed incidents, often improbably linked.*

HEATHCLIFF AND CATHY: ONE REVIEW DESCRIBED EMILY'S TREATMENT OF THEIR RELATIONSHIP AS SHOWING "REAL MASTERY [AND] ... GENIUS."

Shirley was to meet the same objections. The first review proclaimed of the novel:

> *Not one of its men are genuine. There are no such men. There are no <u>Mr Helstones</u>, <u>Mr Yorkes</u>, or <u>Mr Moores</u>. They are all as unreal as Madame Tussaud's waxworks.*

What Victorian society disapproved of it was convenient to dismiss as unreal or improbable. What is astonishing to modern readers is the failure of some contemporary critics to recognize the strong moral purpose of Anne's and Charlotte's novels. Of *Jane Eyre* one critic wrote:

> *... the autobiography of Jane Eyre is pre-eminently an anti-Christian composition. There is throughout it a*

murmuring against the comforts of the rich and against the privations of the poor which ... is a murmuring against God's appointment.

It was the same writer who condemned Currer Bell for making "half our lady readers" enchanted with Rochester for "a model of generosity and honour", although "he is a man who deliberately and secretly seeks to violate the laws both of God and man." She went on, of course, to say that "the popularity of *Jane Eyre* is a proof how deeply the love of the illegitimate romance is implanted in our nature."

Had this been a review of *Wuthering Heights*, it might perhaps have been justified: Heathcliff, despite

his sadism, *is* attractive to "half our lady readers" – although none of them would have seen him as a "model of generosity and honour"! – and his and Catherine's "illegitimate" love meets with no moral censure from Emily; but in *Jane Eyre* Charlotte has Jane making all the "right" moral choices before she can enjoy Rochester's love. He, too, attractive or not, learns, through suffering and self-denial, to accept the constraints of conventional Christian morality in a way that Heathcliff never does.

Wuthering Heights, of course, met with considerable censure as well as puzzled response to its purpose:

> *What may be the moral which the author wishes the reader to deduce from the work it is difficult to say, and … to speak honestly, we have discovered none but mere glimpses of hidden morals or secondary meanings. There seems to us great power in this book, but it is a purposeless power, which we feel a great desire to see turned to better account.*

"COARSENESS"

This Victorian disquiet over the moral purpose of the Brontë novels is matched by the concern over "coarseness". *Jane Eyre* is "stamped with a coarseness of language and laxity of tone" and is marked by "sheer rudeness and vulgarity"; in *Wuthering Heights* "the coarseness extends farther than the mere style; it extends all through", and one reviewer wrote in June 1848:

> *If we did not know that this book has been read by thousands of young ladies in the country, we should esteem it our first duty to caution them against it simply on account of the coarseness of the style … The whole tone of the style of the book smacks of lowness.*

The Tenant of Wildfell Hall, not surprisingly, came in for the same criticisms: it is "one of the coarsest books which we ever perused" and one reviewer, warning "lady readers" not to look at it, talks of the "profane expressions, inconceivably coarse language, and revolting

scenes and descriptions by which its pages are disfigured." Again, the very clear moral intention of the novel is lost in critics' preoccupation with what Edith Wharton would have called the "unpleasant" aspects of life.

Agnes Grey and *The Professor* escaped with little interest or response from the critics. *Villette*, on the other hand, was favourably received: "This book would have made her famous, had she not been so already", wrote one reviewer, and it "amply sustains the fame of the author of *Jane Eyre* and *Shirley*" said another. There were adverse criticisms but they tended to concentrate on the structure or the "bitterness" expressed in the novel rather than on its morality or "coarseness". In contrast to its unfavourable reviews, however, *Jane Eyre* particularly had its great admirers. And there were some contemporaries who recognized the extraordinary "genius" of Emily:

> *The power, indeed is wonderful … It is in the treatment of this subject [Catherine's and Heathcliff's love for each other] that Ellis Bell shows real mastery, and it shows more genius … than you will find in a thousand novels.*

JANE AND ROCHESTER WITH PILOT AND ADÈLE IN THE GARDEN AT THORNFIELD.

CHARLOTTE AND HER PUBLISHERS

CHARLOTTE WAS MOST FORTUNATE in her publishers, unlike Emily and Anne; but in the summer of 1847 her chances of getting a novel into print looked slim. The sisters had already sent the manuscripts of their three novels, *The Professor, Agnes Grey* and *Wuthering Heights*, to a number of publishers before the small company of Newby accepted Emily's and Anne's novels for publication. Whether or not *The Professor* was actually rejected by Newby is not clear; Charlotte's biographers have generally considered it was, but Juliet Barker suggests the decision not to publish with Newby may have been

GEORGE SMITH, THE HANDSOME AND SYMPATHETIC YOUNG DIRECTOR OF SMITH, ELDER AND CO.

Charlotte's because she objected to paying fifty pounds towards the costs, as Emily and Anne agreed to do.

SMITH, ELDER & CO.

The result was fortuitous: Charlotte sent her manuscript to Smith, Elder & Co. Mrs Gaskell describes the state in which it arrived at the firm's address in Cornhill, London:

> *Besides the address to Messrs. Smith, Elder & Co., there were on it those of other publishers to whom the tale had been sent, not obliterated, but simply scored through, so that Mr. Smith at once perceived the names of some of the houses in the trade to which the unlucky parcel had gone, without success …*

Despite the evidence that it had already been rejected several times and although Smith, Elder & Co. declined to publish *The Professor*, their editor, William Smith Williams, wrote such a courteous and encouraging letter to Charlotte that she was spurred on to finish *Jane Eyre*. Smith, Elder published it, Charlotte's second novel, later that year.

Smith Williams was to become an extremely influential person in Charlotte's life. A man with a real love for and sensitivity to literature, he was able to achieve that delicate balance between critical advice and encouragement so important to Charlotte's development as a writer. Smith, Elder kept her supplied with new books, and it was with Smith Williams, in their correspondence, that she discussed her ideas about and responses to much of her reading. To him, too, she poured out her overwhelming sense of loss after the death of Emily. Charlotte's sisters met with no such privileged treatment at the hands of their publishers. In November 1847, Charlotte wrote to Smith Williams contrasting their lot with hers:

Mr Newby … does not do business like Messrs Smith and Elder … [whose] performance is always better than their promise. My relatives have suffered from exhausting delay and procrastination, while I have to acknowledge the benefits of a management, at once business-like and gentlemanlike, energetic and considerate.

There was another very important figure at Smith, Elder, who was to influence Charlotte's life – the young director of the firm, George Smith. It was at the house where he lived with his mother that Charlotte was often entertained when she went to London; and it was George Smith who introduced her to the city's literary and cultural scene. When Anne and Charlotte first travelled to London to reveal their identities to the publishers, he escorted them to the opera and invited them to a grand dinner at his own house.

There is little doubt that George Smith enjoyed entertaining and showing off his new and very successful writer. It is clear, too, that he was sensitive to her emotional needs, offering both support and encouragement after the deaths of her sisters, when she found the finishing of *Shirley* so difficult. He invited her to share holidays with him – in Scotland and on the Rhine; she did actually spend two very happy days with him in Edinburgh.

That Charlotte harboured expectations of more than friendship with George Smith is not surprising. He was young – twenty-five when they met – handsome and sympathetic. She was lonely and very unhappy for much of the time that she knew him. Here was a man who recognized her genius and would encourage her to fulfil it, as well as support her emotionally. But George Smith, in his old age, makes quite plain his feelings for Charlotte in a letter to Mrs Humphrey Ward, which Winifred Gérin quotes in her biography of Charlotte. In it he says that he was never even slightly in love with Charlotte, although he admits

that he thought his mother "rather alarmed" at the prospect. He explains, with some shame, that he was incapable of loving a woman who has "no charm or grace of person", and he states, rather baldly, that Charlotte possessed neither of these qualities. He goes on to say that – when safely separated by distance – he found her interesting and both liked and admired her. The letter certainly suggests, in its reference to the safe distance he preferred between them, that he was aware of Charlotte's attraction to him.

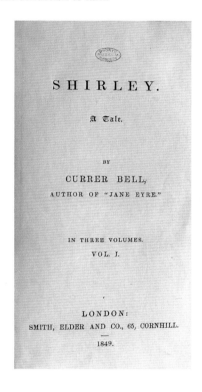

FIRST EDITION OF "SHIRLEY", PUBLISHED BY SMITH, ELDER IN 1849.

In her portrayal of George Smith as Dr John in *Villette*, we see, however, her acceptance of the limits placed on their relationship. When challenged by Smith about what was to happen in the next volume, Charlotte wrote:

Lucy must not marry Dr. John; he is far too youthful, handsome, bright-spirited, and sweet-tempered; he is a "curled darling" of Nature and of Fortune, and must draw a prize in life's lottery. His wife must be young, rich, and pretty …

Lucy Snowe – or, more to the point, Charlotte Brontë – was none of these.

THE GOTHIC AND THE SUPERNATURAL

WALPOLE'S GOTHIC MANSION AT STRAWBERRY HILL.

JANE EYRE AT THORNFIELD HALL — A PLACE FULL OF STRANGE, DEMONIC NOISES.

THE GOTHIC REVIVAL went hand-in-hand with the birth of the Romantic movement in literature. A reaction against eighteenth-century classicism and emphasis on reason, it elevated emotion to the highest place. It was in Horace Walpole's *Anecdotes of Painting*, published in 1764, that we find the Gothic declaration of faith: "One only wants passion to feel Gothic."

It was in his house at Strawberry Hill, Twickenham, which he turned into a mighty Gothic monument, that Horace Walpole wrote his novel *The Castle of Otranto*. In it we find the now familiar Gothic themes and characteristics: mysterious, dark, "sublime" landscape, the turreted mediaeval castle, the prisoner, the demonic hero, the supernatural, suspense.

It is not difficult to recognize here many aspects of the Brontë novels, particularly of *Jane Eyre*, *Villette*, *Wuthering Heights* and *The Tenant of Wildfell Hall*. *Jane Eyre*, for instance, has the Gothic setting of Thornfield Hall, complete with mysterious inhabitant in the attic, of whom Jane becomes aware without knowing her identity. She appears, like "the Vampyre" – but very real – to punish both Rochester and Jane by setting fire to his bed and destroying Jane's wedding-veil. She is both mysterious and mad: Rochester refers to her as a "demon", who emits "the fiercest yells, and the most convulsive plunges." The whole episode in the attic when he reveals Bertha to Jane is calculated to provoke surprise, fear and revulsion in the reader – it evokes these emotions and, in its force, urges us not to question the probabilities with our reason.

Similarly, at the end of the novel, when St John is trying to persuade Jane to marry him so that they can go together as missionaries to India, she hears Rochester calling her. If we are tempted to think she just imagines she hears him, then we are enlightened in the penultimate chapter when he tells her he really did call out those words to her, "If any listener had heard me, he would have thought me mad …" The supernatural, then, reinforces and supports the emotional intensity of the novel, as it does in *Wuthering Heights*.

In Emily's novel, however, the supernatural plays a more complex part. When Lockwood struggles to close the window against the ghost of Cathy who is trying to get in, he is afraid not just of this apparently supernatural image on the outside but also of the elemental, primitive passions which she represents. We know this because we have already been told that Lockwood has a problem with emotional commitment: "While enjoying a month of fine weather at the sea-coast, I was thrown into the company of a most fascinating creature, a real goddess in my eyes, as long as she took no notice of me." His struggles to shut out the young Cathy suggest his desire to keep at bay the passions he can't or won't allow

himself to express. Heathcliff, in contrast, "wrenched open the lattice, bursting, as he pulled at it, into an uncontrollable passion of tears", calling to Cathy to come in as he did so.

There are a number of Gothic elements here: the strange house, with its prison-like bed, the repeated references throughout the scene to supernatural beings or events, "the place was haunted … swarming with ghosts and goblins"; Cathy is "the little fiend … a changeling", "the spectre"; Heathcliff is in the grip of extreme "agitation", behaving like one possessed by some force beyond himself. Outside, "the snow and wind whirled wildly … blowing out the light". Darkness, mystery, suspense and the supernatural are all here, creating a Gothic scene which demands suspension of our reason and the involvement of our emotions.

Nobody reading *Villette* could fail to note the Gothic elements there. Mystery and suspense are built up by the constant references to the ghost of the young nun who haunts the school in Brussels to which Lucy Snowe goes as a teacher. The ghost is of "a girl whom a monkish conclave of the drear middle ages had here buried alive, for some sin against her vow." Gothic writers were especially fond of punishments such as being buried alive for monks or nuns who had broken their vows. Lucy's response to seeing the "nun" in the garret is typically Gothic: the garret itself is "deep, black, cold … ice-cold", and when she sees the apparition, she says "tell me that I was nervous or mad … I cried out; I sickened. Had the shape approached me, I might have swooned …" Suspense in the novel is sustained by other methods, too: the fear engendered in Lucy by the stealth-like Madame Beck, who glides "ghost-like" through the house on her *souliers de silence*. The very "foreignness" of the setting in *Villette* also contributes to its Gothic nature.

There are important Gothic elements in *The Tenant of Wildfell Hall*, too: in the mystery and suspense connected with the identity of Helen Graham and, notably, in the description of Wildfell Hall when she first arrives there: "At length the grim, dark pile appeared before us … We entered the desolate court, and in breathless

anxiety surveyed the ruinous mass. Was it all blackness and desolation?" and the next morning Helen wakens to:

> *The large bare room with its grim old furniture, the narrow, latticed windows, revealing the dull grey sky above and the desolate wilderness below, where the dark stone walls and iron gate, the rank growth of grass and weeds, and the hardy evergreens of preternatural forms, alone remained to tell that there had been once a garden …*

As in all other examples cited here, the effect of this description is an emotional one – we feel with Helen Graham the "breathless anxiety", the "desolation".

A SUITABLY GOTHIC ILLUSTRATION TO A 1931 EDITION OF "WUTHERING HEIGHTS" – CATHY AND HEATHCLIFF ON TOP OF PENISTONE CRAGS.

IMAGERY IN THE NOVELS

IMAGERY CONVEYS MEANING by visual methods. When it works well, it appears and feels quite natural to the reader, reinforcing what the writer is saying and helping to create mood. The repetition of imagery often tends to harden into symbolism, so that the literal often co-exists with the metaphorical. Both Charlotte's and Emily's novels are very rich in imagery and taking a close look at the patterns of the images is a good way to approach their major themes and characters.

In *Jane Eyre*, for instance, images associated with the cold are to be found throughout the novel. When we are first introduced to Jane at her aunt's house, "all was still and petrified under the influence of a hard frost". The cold, of course, is more than a description of a harsh winter: it suggests the lack of human warmth and affection which Jane suffers there. The same is true in early descriptions of Lowood, where the girls suffer the same emotional deprivation.

In contrast, Jane is received at Thornfield by a "cheerful" fire, signifying the emotional warmth which she is going to find in her new home. When Jane discovers the truth about Rochester, however, he anticipates how she will blame him: "you will say, – 'That man had nearly made me his mistress: I must be ice and rock to him;' and ice and rock you will accordingly become." Similarly, Charlotte Brontë repeatedly associates stone and marble images with both Mr Brocklehurst and St John Rivers, who share a common coldness, lacking emotional warmth and passion. In Mr Brocklehurt's case the stone or

ILLUSTRATION FROM A 1943 EDITION OF "JANE EYRE". ROCHESTER AND JANE'S FIRST MEETING.

marble is usually black to convey his evil nature.

Jane Eyre is full of such images, conveying major themes and suggesting the interpretation of the characters. Water, for instance, drowns all Jane's hopes of a fulfilling life with Rochester at the end of Chapter 26, where Jane adapts Psalm 69: "the waters came into my soul; I sank in deep mire: I felt no standing; I came into deep waters; the floods overflowed me." But at the end of the novel, when Jane finds Rochester at Ferndean, the glass of water she takes him suggests the renewed life and hope which she brings.

Images that recur in *Jane Eyre* include birds, light and darkness, storms, food, animals, paradise, the chestnut-tree in the garden at Thornfield, books; they all play a major part in conveying the themes.

The imagery in *Wuthering Heights* works in a similar way. While the elemental themes are the most important, there are other very significant and recurring ones which help with an interpretation of the novel.

BARRIER IMAGES

Windows, when shut, for instance, suggest barriers which separate characters from each other and from their hopes and desires. In the passage where Cathy and Heathcliff look through the drawing-room window at Thrushcross Grange, we see the very different worlds on each side of the window: outside are the moors to which they both naturally belong; inside is the cultivated world of the Lintons, by which Cathy will be seduced. At the end of the passage, she is taken in by the family, and Heathcliff, the unacceptable "gipsy" boy, is left outside. The scene foreshadows what is going to happen in the novel and accentuates the differences between the worlds on either side of the window. When Cathy is dying, she asks Nelly to open the window at Thrushcross Grange:

> Oh, I'm burning! I wish I were out of doors – I wish I were a girl again, half savage, and hardy, and free … Why am I so changed?… I'm sure I should be myself were I once among the heather on those hills. Open the window again wide, fasten it open! Quick, why don't you move?

When Nelly replies that she is afraid of giving Cathy her "death of cold", Cathy retorts, "You won't give me a chance of life, you mean." Cathy knows that the world she rejected is the one which, for her, is life-giving; the open window here, of course, suggests the breaking down of the barriers between her and that world.

When Heathcliff himself dies, at the end of the novel, his window is "swinging open, and the rain driving straight in". In death, all barriers gone, he and the elemental world are united, as he and Cathy are; it is the world to which they naturally belong.

Some other major images in *Wuthering Heights* are gates and doors – which work very much as the windows do – animals, books, hell and the devil.

While in *Villette* we find a similar use of sustained imagery – including storm and tempest, ghosts or the spectral, houses and rooms, and clothes – in *Agnes Grey* and *The Tenant of Wildfell Hall* there is much less evidence of the consistent use of images. Anne does use them, of course, but they tend to be less obvious, less metaphorical or "symbolic".

HEATHCLIFF AND CATHY LOOK THROUGH THE DRAWING-ROOM WINDOW AT THRUSHCROSS GRANGE.

CHARLOTTE'S LETTERS

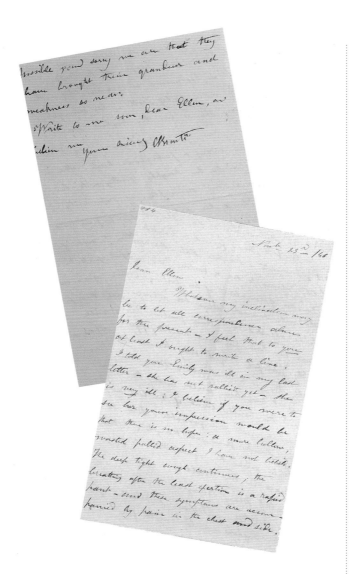

LETTER FROM CHARLOTTE TO ELLEN NUSSEY.

letters, but Ellen failed to do so, leaving us a rich legacy which has provided invaluable insight into the lives of the whole Brontë family. It is likely to provide even more insight when Margaret Smith's most impressive, scholarly edition of the letters is complete.

CHARLOTTE'S CORRESPONDENTS

Letters to Ellen form the vast majority of Charlotte's early correspondence and continue into the last years of her life, despite Ellen's disapproval of Arthur Bell Nicholls as a husband for her friend. Charlotte's other close friend from Roe Head School, the adventurous Mary Taylor, destroyed all but one of Charlotte's letters, an act she was later to regret. And in the years before she was famous there are, of course, the tormented, longing letters Charlotte wrote to Monsieur Heger, pleading with him to reply.

To the period after the publication of *Jane Eyre* belongs a number of important new correspondents, chief among them, perhaps, being her editor, William Smith Williams, and her publisher, George Smith, at Smith, Elder & Co. There were letters, too, to such prominent figures as Mrs Gaskell, and to those less prominent, like one written from London and quoted by Mrs Gaskell in her *Life of Charlotte Brontë*, to the Parsonage servant, Martha:

> *It appears, from a letter I received from Papa this morning, that you are now all in the bustle of unroofing; and I look with much anxiety at a somewhat clouded sky, hoping and trusting that it will not rain till all is covered in.*

REGRETTABLY, THERE ARE very few extant letters from Charlotte's siblings. In contrast, there are hundreds of letters by Charlotte, including the three hundred and eighty "intimate and revealing ones", as Margaret Smith describes them, to Ellen Nussey. As we have already seen, Arthur Bell Nicholls asked Ellen to destroy all of Charlotte's

You and Martha Redman are to take care not to break your backs with attempting to lift and carry heavy weights; also you are not foolishly to run into draughts, go out without caps and bonnets, or otherwise take measures to make yourselves ill. I was rather curious to know how you have managed about a sleeping place for yourself and Tabby.

The sheer variety of Charlotte's letters makes fascinating reading. In them she includes details of her daily life, reading, thoughts and feelings. It is interesting to note how she adapts her style and tone to her audience. Four days after Emily's death she writes to Ellen:

She is gone, after a hard, short conflict … there is no Emily in time or on earth now. Yesterday we put her poor, wasted, mortal frame quietly under the church pavement … We feel she is at peace. No need now to tremble for the hard frost and the keen wind. Emily does not feel them. She died in a time of promise.

Here she states the facts simply and clearly for an old friend who knew Emily from girlhood. In her letter to William Smith Williams, Charlotte describes the loss of Emily in more graphic and emotive terms:

Emily is nowhere here now … we have laid her cherished head under the church aisle beside my mother's, my two sisters', dead long ago, and my poor, hapless brother's …

Here her head is "cherished" and the list of her family already buried emphasizes the cumulative loss which Emily's death represents for her. Why does she write so differently to these two friends? Is it that she feels a special need at this moment in her life for Williams' sympathy? Does the fact that he is her editor influence her style? Is she writing for a publisher here? Certainly, the letter to Williams is strikingly more "poetic", more conscious of literary effect than her letter to Ellen:

… the loss is ours – not hers, and some sad comfort I take, as I hear the wind blow and feel the cutting keen-

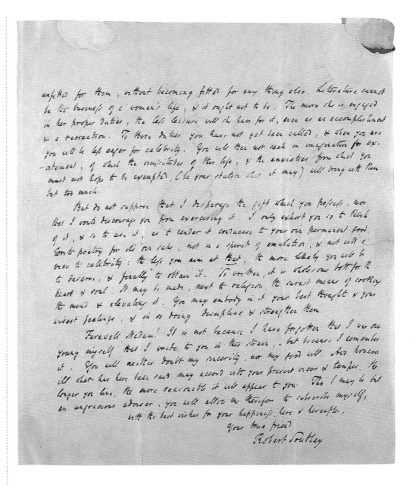

ness of the frost, in knowing that the elements bring her no more suffering … her fever is quieted, her restlessness soothed, her deep, hollow cough is hushed for ever …

The rhythm, the repetition in the structure of the phrasing, the strong visual effect caused by the elemental imagery all suggest a "literary" awareness absent in her letter to Ellen.

THE COMPLETE LETTERS

Charlotte's letters have suffered various indignities. Not only have many, like those to Mary Taylor, been destroyed, but, after her death, both Patrick and Arthur Bell Nicholls resorted to cutting up into fragments some of her original letters to satisfy autograph-hunters. Problems with the editing and collating of the letters have abounded, which is why it is particularly encouraging to see coming into print a complete, thorough and accurate edition.

"LITERATURE CANNOT BE THE BUSINESS OF A WOMAN'S LIFE: AND IT OUGHT NOT TO BE." THE POET, ROBERT SOUTHEY'S FAMOUS REPLY TO A LETTER CHARLOTTE WROTE TO HIM ASKING HIS OPINION OF HER LITERARY TALENTS.

THE DIARY PAPERS

SKETCH BY EMILY OF

THE TWO SISTERS

WRITING THEIR DIARY

PAPER, JUNE 26,

1837. ANNE IS

FACING US, EMILY

HAS HER BACK TO US.

O F CHARLOTTE WE KNOW a great deal through both her letters and Mrs Gaskell's *Life*, but the latter includes no first-hand information of the younger siblings since Mrs Gaskell never met them. The diary papers, exclusively Emily's and Anne's creations, are therefore particularly valuable because they allow us to meet Emily and Anne and see,

through their eyes, the family, life at the Parsonage and their hopes for the future.

The five diary papers were written to be opened and read several – usually four – years later. The first is written by both sisters together, one is by Anne alone, and three by Emily alone. Two of them are illustrated with sketches. They all reveal a number of very important things about the Brontës' lives.

TEENAGE REBELLION

The first thing that strikes the reader, perhaps, is the atrocious spelling and punctuation of the first one, written in November 1834 when Emily was sixteen. The effect, though, is striking: it has an immediacy that a work written for a public audience can rarely have. It is the obvious spontaneous recording not only of events in the Parsonage but also of what is happening in their Gondal world and of the fact that Robert Peel is going to be asked "to stand for Leeds". Perhaps even more interestingly, it gives us an insight into the girls' characters:

> *it is past Twelve o'clock Anne / and I have not tided*
> *ourselvs, done our / bed work [or] done*
> *our lessons and we / want to go out to play …*
> *Anne and I have not Done our music …*

Here is the voice of teenage rebellion against adult authority – to be found also in Anne's answer to Aunt Branwell's "where are your feet /Anne Anne answered on the floor Aunt".

The diary papers reveal a very closely knit and interdependent family, in which Branwell is a vital and

integral participant in the early examples. In the first, Patrick comes into the parlour and gives him a letter which he is to show his aunt and Charlotte. In the second – written by Emily in June 1837 – Branwell is reading to Charlotte while she is working in her aunt's room.

By 1841, they are all separated, Emily at home, Charlotte and Anne governesses – the latter in Scarborough – and Branwell "a clerk in the railroad station at Luddenden Foot." Both Anne and Emily's diary papers exist for this date, and both mention the sisters hoping to set up their own school. Emily looks forward to Patrick, her aunt and Branwell coming to visit them there. By the last diary paper, however, in 1845 Emily records that all are well "with the exception of B., who, I hope, will be better and do better hereafter." Her entry that "Anne left her situation at Thorp Green of her own accord" suggests a contrast with Branwell's dismissal from his post there probably only some ten days before the diary paper was written.

What all the diary papers show is how readily the sisters move between their actual day-to-day lives and the imaginary world of Gondal, often in the same sentence. It is a strange kind of dual existence, since the actual world is catalogued very precisely. Emily writes, for instance, that in four years' time: "Charlotte will be 25 and 2 months … myself 22 and 10 months" and, on another occasion, "C. and I returned from Brussels, November 8th, 1842, in consequence of aunt's death". Was her hold on the actual world sometimes so tenuous that she felt the need to pin it down with great precision? Yet she is clearly happy and at home in her domestic work: peeling potatoes and "tidying our desk boxes"; in her 1845 diary paper, she writes:

I am quite contented for myself: not as idle as formerly, altogether as hearty, and having learnt to make the most of the present … seldom or never troubled with nothing to do, and merely desiring that everybody could be as comfortable as myself and as undesponding, and then we should have a very tolerable world of it … I must hurry off now to my turning and ironing. I have plenty of work on hands, and writing, and am altogether full of business.

By the time she wrote this, all the sisters were back home in the Parsonage, and Emily writes with some relief, "Our school scheme has been abandoned … Now I don't desire a school at all, and none of us have any great longing for it." It is clear that Emily is quite happy combining her imaginative and domestic worlds in the security of her own home.

For Anne, as her diary paper of 1841 shows, things were rather different. On holiday with the Robinson family at Scarborough, she looks forward to "many a weary week" before she will see her sisters again. Nevertheless, with typical soul-searching, she talks of having "more wisdom and experience, and a little more self-possession" than at the time of writing the last diary paper.

Like Emily, she wonders what the future holds. Designed to be read later, the diary papers repeatedly refer to the years ahead, adding a particular poignancy to them now:

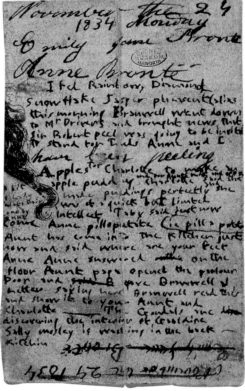

I wonder what will be our condition and how or where we shall all be on this day four years hence …

This day four years I wonder whether we shall still be dragging on in our present condition or established to our hearts' content. Time will show.

In the first diary paper Emily had looked forward to the year 1874, "in which year / I shall be in my 57th year / Anne will be going in her 55th / year … hoping we / shall all be well at that time." She concludes her last one, to be opened on her thirtieth birthday: "With best wishes for the whole house till 1848, July 30th, and as much longer as maybe." There was not to be much longer: she died the following December.

THE DIARY PAPERS

THE ART OF THE BRONTËS

WATERCOLOUR OF A
BLUE CONVOLVULUS,
BY CHARLOTTE,
C. DECEMBER 1832.

ART PLAYED AN IMPORTANT role in the lives of all the Brontës, and was a hobby throughout their lives. In the early years, their pictures went hand in hand with their creative writing: descriptions of the heroes and heroines of the juvenilia were based on the printed images of great men and lovely ladies in the illustrated annuals and books which found their way onto the bookshelves of Haworth Parsonage. Exotic scenes of pillared temples and apocalyptic Biblical visions were conjured up not just from the imagination but also from the prints of pictures by the Romantic artist John Martin (1789–1854) which hung on the walls of their father's study. Popular prints of famous paintings by Landseer and Etty sowed the seeds of inspiration for many a tale.

Charlotte, of all the Brontë children, was the most obsessed with art, developing an early ambition to be an artist. She toiled away at her meticulous copies of landscapes, flowers, society ladies and Byronic heroines; and when she was just eighteen years old she had her drawings of Bolton and Kirkstall Abbeys exhibited at the annual exhibition of the Northern Society for the Encouragement of the Fine Arts in Leeds. All the family went to see them on display, alongside works by the local portrait painter, William Robinson, who became Branwell's tutor. In the days when the odds were stacked against women having a career of any kind, however, there was little hope of Charlotte ever realizing her dream of becoming a professional artist. The most she would do with her drawing skills would be to use them in her work as a governess.

In Charlotte's novels, art is a recurring theme, especially in *Jane Eyre*. The novel opens with Jane looking at a book by Bewick – an artist whose birds and animals the Brontës copied freely. Later, at Thornfield, Rochester flips through Jane's portfolio, making provocative remarks about her drawings. We also see Jane, depressed by her own plainness in contrast to Blanche Ingram's beauty, sitting down to paint a delicate watercolour miniature of Blanche, while she paints herself on rough paper and with thick charcoal, calling the image "Portrait of a governess, disconnected, poor and plain". Branwell, being the only boy, had more opportunities open to him to develop his artistic flair, and the plan was that he should go to the Royal Academy of Arts in London to study at the schools there. He never made the grade even to apply, however, and the story that he went to London in pursuit of an artist's career has been disproved. The most he ever achieved was a mere twelve months practice as a portrait painter in Bradford, where the lure of bohemian company in the public houses of the city swiftly distracted him from his career. Branwell did have a natural talent for drawing; indeed, he would have made a competent cartoonist, as his many sketches of his friends and his numerous denigrating self-portraits suggest.

Despite his conspicuous lack of success as an artist in his lifetime, two paintings by Branwell in London's National Portrait Gallery are today probably the most famous portraits of writers in the world: his group portrait of the Brontë sisters and the portrait of Emily, torn from another group portrait, the rest of which is long since destroyed. The former is a haunting image of the young Brontës, each of them staring out of the picture in characteristic fashion – Charlotte with fierce determination, Anne with a dreaming look, and Emily abstracted in her own world.

Emily's drawings from life of her animals, notably her beloved dogs, Grasper and Keeper, show a natural facility for observational drawing, clearly born out of deep affection for her pets. Her copies from prints – of saints, birds and female faces – are, by contrast, impatient and inconsistent, unlike Charlotte's careful, minutely detailed efforts. In her diary paper illustrations Emily also left us the only sketches of the Brontë sisters at work, writing together around the dining-room table. Like Branwell, she made a number of rapid self-portrait sketches, thumbnail studies of the writer squatting on her little wooden stool with her writing-desk on her knee and the faithful Keeper lying at her side.

Anne, as the youngest of the family, was as often the model as the artist. When she was very small, her brother and sisters made little books and drawings for her, and it is clear that she began to join in the creativity as soon as she could manage a pencil. Charlotte drew

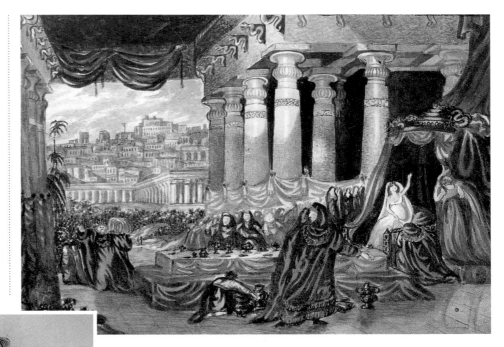

her several times, making her sit with a shawl draped across her shoulders in the classical manner, or wearing the red carnelian beads which survive at the Parsonage today. In her twenties Anne made a self-portrait, gazing rapt into the mirror, giving herself lustrous curls and enormous eyes. We know that, as a governess at Thorpe Green in the early 1840s, she enjoyed wandering the grounds with her sketch-pad, and she has left us a number of beautiful studies of trees and landscape. In *The Tenant of Wildfell Hall*, of course, her heroine is not only an artist but even makes money from her paintings. Much of Anne's own delight in nature is expressed in Helen Huntingdon's thoughts and words.

THE ARTISTIC LEGACY

The Brontës' drawings and watercolours, and Branwell's portraits in oils, many of which survive today and may be seen at the Parsonage Museum, make a very valuable contribution to our understanding and appreciation of their lives and their creative vision.

"QUEEN ESTHER", BRANWELL'S WATERCOLOUR COPY, 1830, OF THE PRINT OF ESTHER'S FEAST BY JOHN MARTIN.

CHARLOTTE'S PORTRAIT IN PENCIL OF ANNE, APRIL 17TH 1833. IT HAS BEEN DESCRIBED AS "AN EXCELLENT LIKENESS OF ANNE BRONTË."

THE ART OF THE BRONTËS

3 THE LANDSCAPE OF THE BRONTËS

WHEN CONJURING UP AN IMAGE of the Brontës, most of us place them in Haworth, on the edge of the moors. While that is, indeed, the place which they called home and where they rightfully belong – both physically and emotionally – other places, too, either contributed to the forming of the family's attitudes and characteristics or had a direct influence on the members of the family who went there.

Perhaps most important of all to bear in mind when we read the Brontës is that they were pure Celts, with an Irish father and a Cornish mother. To that background can be attributed many of their characteristics as a family: their emotional intensity, kept well under control much of the time, as well as their love of nature and of animals. These are not, of course, attributes solely of the Celtic race, but they are likely to have been inherited from or fostered by the Brontë parents, Patrick in particular. It is difficult to assess how much the very important political and social events taking place in Ireland between 1790 and 1850 affected the Brontës.

The sisters' visits to London clearly made a very important impression on Charlotte. Before she had been to the city herself, she wrote to Ellen, "You have returned or are returning from London – from the great city which is to me as apocryphal as Babylon, or Nineveh or ancient Rome." In an earlier letter she had referred to it as "the mercantile metropolis of Europe." Mercantile it may have been, but its political, historical and cultural significance in particular drew Charlotte to London.

Belgium, of course, was of paramount importance in furnishing Charlotte with the setting for both *The Professor* and *Villette*. There are detailed descriptions in both these novels of the physical, educational, religious and social differences between Belgium and England, which serve to accentuate the isolation of her characters. For the young women arriving from Yorkshire, Brussels must have seemed both a daunting and fascinating place, although Emily seems to have been singularly unaffected by it.

There are other places of significance to Charlotte, who enjoyed visiting both her old school friends and the new ones she made as a famous writer. The Lake District could not have failed to move her, being the inspiration for so many poets who, in their turn, had inspired her.

It was Anne who fell in love with the sea and wanted to see it again before her death. Scarborough – or some spot in its vicinity – must, one feels, have been the inspiration for the scene in *Agnes Grey* where Mr Weston proposes to Agnes: "a bold hill on the land side, and towards the sea, a steep precipice, from the summit of which a glorious view is to be had." Anne was to describe, in more detail, a similar scene in *The Tenant of Wildfell Hall*.

Haworth and the moors above it – shown opposite in summer – are many miles from the sea that Anne loved, but for Emily they encompassed all that she wanted, as is so clearly evident in the imagery of both *Wuthering Heights* and her poems.

IRELAND

THE RUGGED, BEAUTIFUL LANDSCAPE OF THE WEST OF IRELAND.

❝OF ALL THE DOCTRINES [Patrick] preached to the men of Erin the Irish found that forgiveness of injuries was the hardest, and the nation in this respect seems unchanged to this day." These words are not, of course, about Patrick Brontë, but about St Patrick, for whom Mr Brontë was named; and they were not written in our own time, but by Lady Wilde, the mother of Oscar Wilde. They are a poignant reminder of the conflict which has raged in that beautiful country for so long.

It was a conflict familiar in Patrick Brontë's own family. His younger brother, William, was a United Irishman, dedicated to making Ireland a republic and ending its traditional and turbulent connection with England. It was in 1791 that Wolfe Tone, a dynamic and influential Protestant leader, had founded the first club of the Society of United Irishmen in Belfast.

POLITICAL UPHEAVAL

When political and nationalist frustrations reached their peak with the 1798 rising, Patrick was twenty-one years old – teaching at Drumballyroney school and, later, tutor to the Reverend Thomas Tighe's children. He cannot have been without knowledge of or, indeed, opinions on these momentous political events – his brother fought with the rebel forces in one of the battles of 1798 – but there is no record of his views at the time.

Events which have taken on mythical significance in Irish history took place when Patrick was in his twenties: the French fleet arriving off the west coast of Ireland to help in the republican cause, the atrocities on both sides in Wexford, the deaths of his fellow Protestants – Wolfe Tone, Robert Emmet, Edward Fitzgerald – all in the nationalist cause.

We do not know what he thought about all these. We do know that he was a strong supporter of the Act of Union of 1801, which created the United Kingdom of Great Britain and Ireland; but then so, at the time, were many Catholic Irish, anticipating their emancipation in its wake. That he abhorred violence and disorder is clear, and by the 1840s he was sufficiently concerned about civil war in Ireland to write to his brother about the need for resisting, with force if necessary, Catholic pressure to repeal the Act of Union.

Although Ireland was used to deprivation, poverty and injustice, the 1840s saw suffering on a scale not witnessed before. Just as the introduction of machinery into the mills in England caused unemployment and Luddite resistance, so the increasing mechanization of the Irish linen and woollen factories led to the loss of jobs on a massive scale in Ireland. For an already impoverished people this was disastrous; but worse was to follow.

THE POTATO FAMINE

The staple diet of Ireland was the potato; easily grown and tended, it was capable of being produced in quantity on very small patches of land. Nutritious and filling, it kept the Irish peasant well fed, better nourished than his English counterpart on a wheat-based diet. It has been established that the Irish were consuming seven million tonnes of potatoes a year by the 1840s.

There had been failure of the potato crop before, but in isolated pockets of Ireland and of no great duration. In 1845, however, a new blight occurred and spread throughout the country; in 1846 it reached catastrophic proportions – nearly four million people were threatened with starvation unless England could organize a massive relief programme. The tragic story of the next few years is well known. Despite some heroic efforts to alleviate the suffering, too little action, too late led to unimaginable suffering among vast numbers of the Irish people, particularly in Connacht in the far west. By 1848, in one area of County Clare one out of every twenty people was dying of starvation or the diseases which accompanied the famine.

With the threat of starvation came another: that of eviction. If you could not pay your rent, then you were likely to be put out of your house; and the history of the late 1840s records the lot of hundreds of thousands of Irish peasants left to die in the fields or by the roadside or, if they were lucky, in the workhouses – often too full to accommodate them.

CHARLOTTE AND IRELAND

Fear of such a fate led, of course, to mass emigration – to England, America and Australia. The legacy of the famine has been far-reaching – the Irish memory, both at home and across the world, carries the depth and bitterness of its suffering to this day. When Charlotte Brontë was writing of Jane Eyre's physical and emotional deprivation at Lowood, was she aware of events across the Irish Sea, where her father was born, or, indeed, in those "coffin ships" carrying Irish emigrants?

She was herself, of course, to marry an Irishman and to spend her honeymoon in Ireland less than ten years after these events. Of Mr Nicholls' family household in Banagher, she wrote – revealing her English prejudices, despite her Irish ancestry – "I was … greatly surprised to find so much of English order and repose in the family habits and arrangements." The scenery, too, surpassed all her expectations, as well it might. Cecil Woodham-Smith, in *The Great Hunger*, talks of how difficult it must have been for emigrants from the west of Ireland to leave one of the most beautiful places in the world to go to the big cities of America or Australia. A lover of the Yorkshire moors could not fail to be moved by the landscapes of Connacht. How sad that Emily never went there and saw them for herself!

PATRICK BRONTË'S BIRTHPLACE IN IRELAND.

IRELAND

CORNWALL

MARIA BRANWELL, the Brontës' mother, was born in one of the most beautiful and most remote parts of England. Narrow lanes wind through verdant countryside, never far from the sea, while high cliffs and hidden coves form England's western boundary. Even now, with the car and train at our disposal, it is not difficult for us to imagine what the journey to Cornwall must have been like for travellers in the eighteenth and nineteenth centuries.

According to John Davy's biography of his famous brother, Sir Humphry Davy, at the time of their mother's girlhood in Penzance in about 1770, there were no proper roads in Cornwall. People travelled almost exclu-

sively on horseback, and goods were transported by packhorse, using bridlepaths which crisscrossed the county. In Penzance itself, their mother related, there existed only one cart, and houses were very simply furnished, with sea-salt sprinkled on the floors instead of carpets.

John Davy speaks of the extreme ignorance of the "lower class" and the superstition of all the inhabitants at this time, as well as of the drunkenness and "low scale of morals" of the middle and upper classes. Smuggling, a traditional Cornish occupation, flourished: in 1778, according to one letter-writer, "Irish wherries carrying 14, 16 or more guns and well-manned frequently land many large quantities of goods in defiance of the officers of Customs and Excise, and their crews armed with swords and pistols escort the smugglers a considerable distance from the sea." Military force was often required to deal with such incidents.

Because of its coastal position and its proximity to France, Cornwall has always been vulnerable to attack; the history of the county is full of requests for government support in soldiers and weaponry with which to defend itself. On and off, from the end of the seventeenth century to 1815, England was at war with France, and Cornwall was constantly on the alert against invasion.

THE RUGGED COASTLINE OF CORNWALL.

THE BRANWELLS OF PENZANCE

Those writing about life in Penzance in the last decades of the eighteenth century and the first of the nineteenth see a marked change from the world of John Davy's mother, and most, if not all, attribute that change to the advent and spread of Methodism. The Branwells themselves were Methodists and the young Maria – and her sister Elizabeth – must have grown up aware of the worldly vices their parents decried. It is very probable that the future Mrs Brontë actually heard John Wesley preach on his last visit to the town in 1789, when she was six years old. The Wesley brothers had been preaching in Cornwall since 1743, and their influence, although taking hold but gradually, was widespread and deep-rooted: the Methodists' opposition to drunkenness, swearing, gambling and smuggling resulted eventually in a decline in all these vices after the first decades of the nineteenth century.

The Penzance of Maria's childhood and young adulthood was, by all accounts, prosperous. Tin-mining and fishing were Cornwall's chief industries, and tin and fish her main exports: pilchards – extremely plentiful in the summer – were sent as far afield as Portugal and Spain. A successful trading town, Penzance was becoming the heart of Cornwall's banking as well a social centre: in 1791 it built its own Assembly Room, and it is here in 1805, according to legend, that news of Nelson's victory at Trafalgar was first announced in England.

Even before Maria's birth the Ladies' Book Club had been established in the town, to be followed by the Gentlemen's Book Club and News Room and, reflecting some concern for the less privileged in their society, by the Penzance Public Dispensary and Humane Society, which provided the poor with medical advice and help. Maria and Elizabeth grew up in changing times: while their cultural world was expanding, when war with France broke out again in 1793, trade – on which the town and their father were so dependent – must have been more precarious. Nevertheless, it is clear that their memories of their birthplace were extremely happy. Mrs Gaskell records

how Maria – at the end of her life – asked her nurse "to raise her in bed to let her see her clean the grate, 'because she did it as it was done in Cornwall'".

FROM PENZANCE TO YORKSHIRE

In writing of the changes which Elizabeth Branwell had to adjust to when she arrived in Haworth, Mrs Gaskell talks of the mild climate enjoyed by Penzance, "where plants which we in the north call greenhouse flowers grow in great profusion, and without any shelter even in the winter, and where the soft warm climate allows the inhabitants, if so disposed, to live pretty constantly in the open air." She recognizes how hard it must have been "for a lady considerably past forty" to come to Yorkshire and "take up her abode in a place where neither flowers nor vegetables would flourish, and where a tree of even moderate dimensions might be hunted for far and wide." The Penzance of her description is the attractive resort which writers, even in the Branwell sisters' youth, were recommending as a fitting place for invalids to visit – for the very reasons that Mrs Gaskell gives. It was not just the climate, however, that Aunt Branwell regretted leaving behind in Cornwall: "She missed the small round of cheerful, social visiting perpetually going on in a country town". No doubt Maria did, too.

ST MICHAEL'S MOUNT, JUST OFFSHORE PENZANCE.

BRONTË COUNTRY

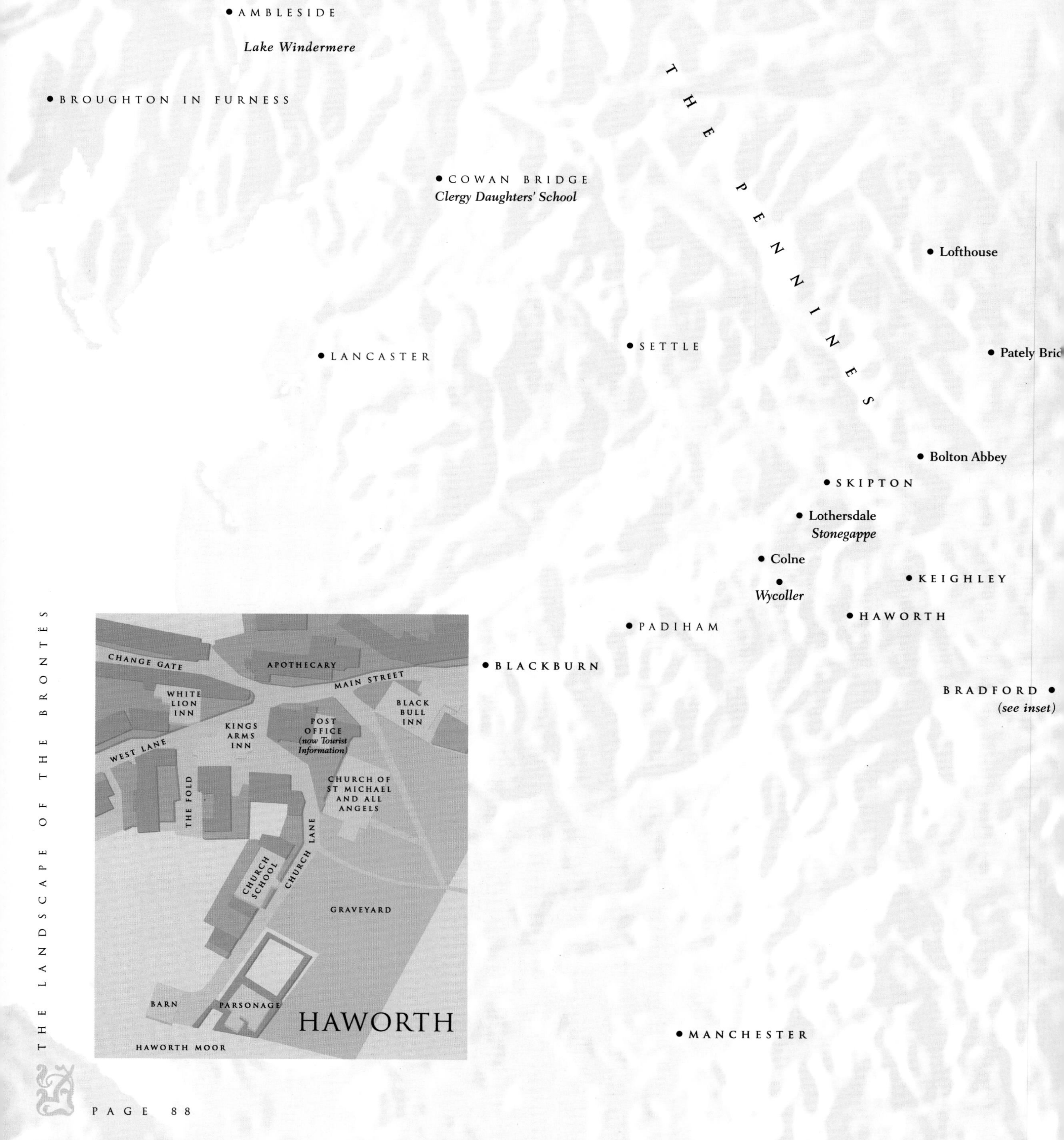

●AMBLESIDE

Lake Windermere

●BROUGHTON IN FURNESS

●COWAN BRIDGE
Clergy Daughters' School

●LANCASTER

●SETTLE

T H E   P E N N I N E S

●Lofthouse

●Pately Brid

●Bolton Abbey

●SKIPTON

●Lothersdale
Stonegappe

●Colne

Wycoller

●KEIGHLEY

●HAWORTH

●PADIHAM

●BLACKBURN

BRADFORD ●
(see inset)

CHANGE GATE

APOTHECARY

MAIN STREET

WHITE
LION
INN

BLACK
BULL
INN

KINGS
ARMS
INN

POST
OFFICE
*(now Tourist
Information)*

WEST LANE

THE FOLD

CHURCH OF
ST MICHAEL
AND ALL
ANGELS

CHURCH SCHOOL

CHURCH LANE

GRAVEYARD

BARN

PARSONAGE

HAWORTH

HAWORTH MOOR

●MANCHESTER

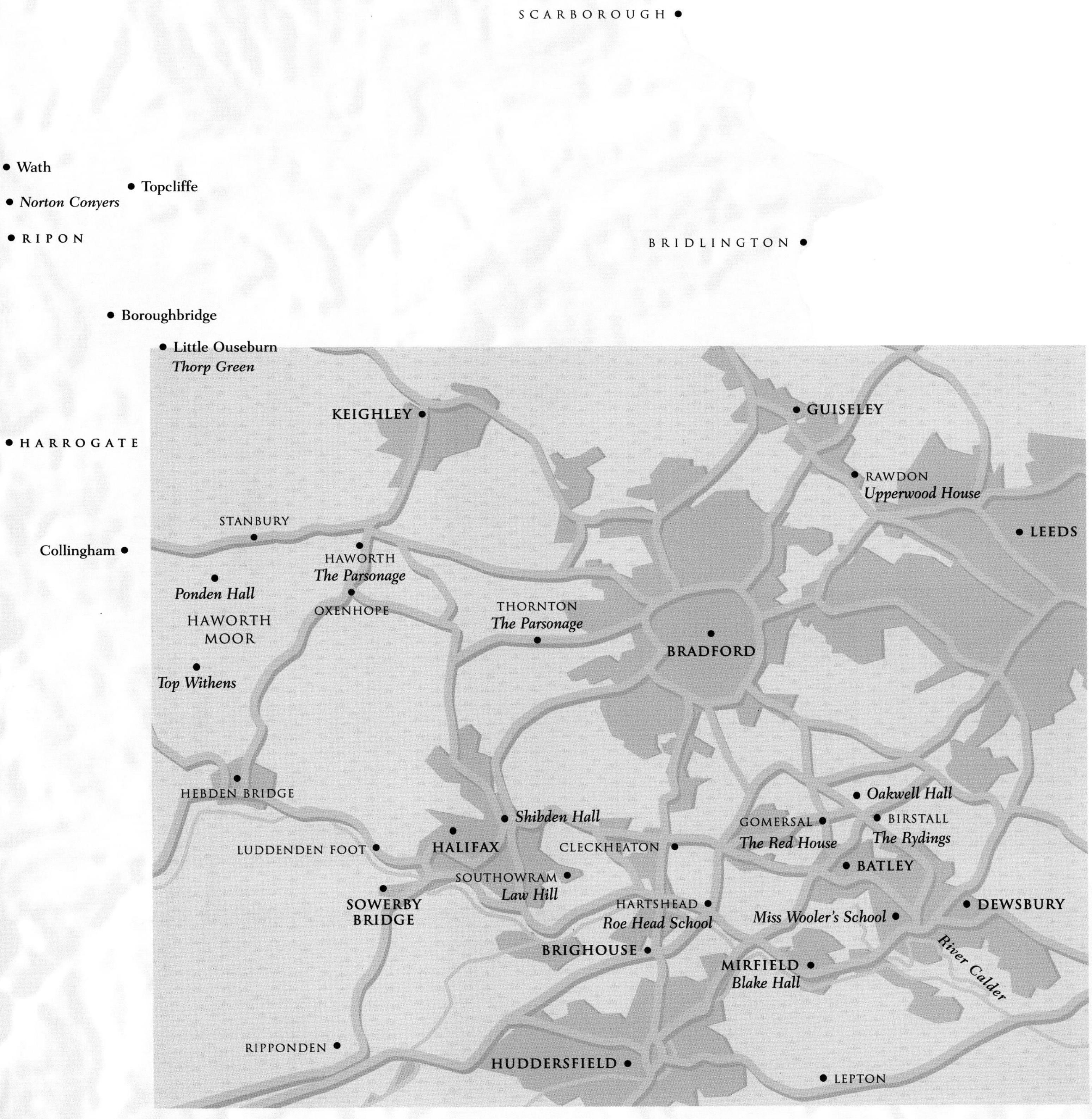

SCARBOROUGH •

• Wath
• Topcliffe
• Norton Conyers

• RIPON

BRIDLINGTON •

• Boroughbridge

• Little Ouseburn
Thorp Green

KEIGHLEY •

• GUISELEY

• HARROGATE

• RAWDON
Upperwood House

STANBURY

• LEEDS

Collingham •

HAWORTH
The Parsonage

Ponden Hall

OXENHOPE

HAWORTH
MOOR

THORNTON
The Parsonage

BRADFORD

Top Withens

HEBDEN BRIDGE

Oakwell Hall

Shibden Hall

BIRSTALL
The Rydings

GOMERSAL
The Red House

LUDDENDEN FOOT •

HALIFAX

CLECKHEATON

BATLEY

SOUTHOWRAM
Law Hill

SOWERBY
BRIDGE

HARTSHEAD
Roe Head School

Miss Wooler's School

• DEWSBURY

River Calder

BRIGHOUSE

MIRFIELD
Blake Hall

RIPPONDEN

HUDDERSFIELD

LEPTON

• SHEFFIELD

• HATHERSAGE

HAWORTH

OOKING OUT FROM the top of the church tower at Haworth, one can see the whole village, dropping down from the hilltop where its centre lies and up the other side of the valley towards Keighley. Below are the mills; above the village sweep the moors.

Approaching the Parsonage from Keighley, as Mrs Gaskell did in 1853, the modern traveller is struck, as she was, by the steepness of the hill that leads into the village, where the flagstones are "placed end-ways, in order to give a better hold to the horses' feet; and, even with this help, they seem to be in constant danger of slipping backwards." The stone houses on either side of the road are terraced, their front doors reached by steps up from the road, an indication of the cellars beneath a number of them.

At the top of the hill lies the heart of the village – to the left the Black Bull, a favourite haunt of Branwell, and behind it the church. In this small area are a couple more pubs and a few houses and shops, among them the apothecary's where Branwell bought his drugs. The Parsonage is to be found up a short lane behind the church and beyond the graveyard.

THE BABBAGE REPORT

We have a very detailed picture of what the village was like in 1850 because, in that year, was published a report to the General Board of Health on "the Sewerage, Drainage, and Supply of Water, and the Sanitary Condition of the Inhabitants of the Hamlet of HAWORTH". The inspector in charge of the inquiry was Benjamin Babbage. His observations and conclusions were – and remain – shocking.

Haworth's size, perhaps, suggests more a town than a village: Babbage calls it both. At the time of his Report, there were three spinning and weaving mills in the village, employing surprisingly few people – just over two hundred. Most of the people of Haworth worked, however, in their own homes, combing wool for the mills. Babbage observes:

OLD HAWORTH, WITH ITS STEEP FLAGSTONED HILL.

In order to obtain the proper temperature for this opera-tion, iron stoves are fixed in the rooms where it is carried on, which are kept alight day and night, and the win-dows are seldom, if ever, opened, excepting in the height of summer. In some cases I found that this business was carried on in bed-rooms, which consequently became very close and unhealthy …

The working conditions, then, of many of the people were not only unpleasant; they were actively contribut-ing to ill-health. Although the very high mortality rate in Haworth must have been obvious to the inhabitants, it was not until the Babbage Report was published that the exact figures were known.

Over the twelve years between 1838 and 1849 the average age at death was 25.8, comparable to some of the most unhealthy districts of London. In fact, 41.6 per cent of the population of Haworth died before reaching the age of six. The churchyard bears plentiful evidence of this high death rate among children – one headstone commemorates eleven children who died in infancy. In a report which is, by its nature, concerned with facts and figures, Babbage shows his humanity when he com-ments that "where this amount of infantile mortality prevails, who shall picture the mother's anxious care for her drooping offspring, the father's hard tasked labour to provide his family with the needful food and medicines", and he expresses his concern for the surviving children struggling to have "an average chance of life". Such a picture makes the Brontës' lives seem positively long!

SANITATION

The working conditions were clearly a contributory fac-tor to this high death rate, but there were other much more serious problems. The sanitary state of the village was appalling. In some instances one privy was shared by the inhabitants of twenty-four houses – Babbage speaks here of the offence to decency as well as the dangers to health, since several of the privies were in clear public view. He describes the middens, where refuse, including "night soil", piled up against the houses and seeped

through the walls – piles standing sometimes for a couple of months, building up below windows and emitting the most offensive smells. The middens often included offal from the slaughter-houses. There were no sewers in the village; drainage was mostly in open channels running along the road.

Clearly here was a real need for the installation of proper sewerage and drain-age and the provision of unpolluted water, such as Edwin Chadwick recom-mended everywhere. In Haworth not only was there insufficient water for the needs of the population at that time, but much of it was polluted by the lack of proper drainage and sewage disposal. Those living in cel-lar-rooms, below the level of

the road, were especially vulnerable; but the whole vil-lage was affected, too, by the position of the graveyard. It was, by 1850, already very full – 1,344 burials in the previous ten years, all of them visible from the Parsonage windows. The flat stones lying horizontally on top of the bodies and the lack of drainage meant contamination of the water supply. Babbage recom-mended the immediate closure of the graveyard and the installation of "air-tight pipes into the main sewer", as well as all the drastic improvements needed in the vil-lage as a whole, including an adequate number of privies, the provision of drainage and sewerage, the building of a reservoir, and the piping of water to every house.

Despite Branwell's contribution to the alcoholic intake of Haworth, surprisingly Babbage found that "the total consumption of beer and spirituous liquors … is very much below the average of other places." One won-ders why. Was Patrick more successful in restraining his parishioners than he was his son?

HAWORTH TODAY,
CLEARLY RECOGNIZABLE
BUT LESS DOUR THAN
IN THE PAST.

HAWORTH

THE MOORS

THE MOORS, when the Brontës were alive, were much more densely inhabited than they are today, as the ruined remains of old stone farmhouses dotted across the landscape testify. There was sheep-farming, of course, and cattle and horses grazed the lower moorland. It was a hard life for those who worked the land, especially on the higher slopes, and many eked out some kind of living with cottage crafts, like wool-combing and hand-weaving.

PURE AND BRACING

Not far out of the village were the Pennistone quarries, which employed large numbers of Haworth men. The stone had to be quarried and transported locally for the building of houses, walls, mills and roads; it was a very valuable commodity. The disused quarries are a distinctive feature of the moorland landscape today.

TOP WITHENS, THE NOW RUINED FARMHOUSE ON TOP OF THE MOOR, WHICH WAS PROBABLY THE INSPIRATION FOR THE SITE OF WUTHERING HEIGHTS.

Beyond them, higher up, lie the vast stretches of peat and bog which were clearly Heathcliff's and Cathy's domain. They are remarkably unchanged since the Brontës' day, although there would have been much more evidence of habitation in the first half of the nineteenth century, and cart tracks would have criss-crossed the moor connecting the various farms and cottages. It is here that we find the ruined farmhouse, Top Withens, which has traditionally been associated with the site for *Wuthering Heights*. Emily describes the setting of the house:

Pure, bracing ventilation they must have up there, at all times, indeed: one may guess the power of the north wind, blowing over the edge, by the excessive slant of a few stunted firs at the end of the house; and by a range of gaunt thorns all stretching their limbs one way, as if craving alms of the sun. Happily, the architect had foresight to build it strong: the narrow windows are deeply set in the wall, and the corners defended with large jutting stones.

The landscape captures the imagination with its primitive, elemental power. In winter the vast, panoramic expanse is covered in snow; in summer the purple heather sweeps across the rounded hills and down into the valleys, where the streams, water tinged with brown from the peat above, wind their way between high banks and under stone bridges. One may still find harebells hidden among the grass in obscure parts of the moor, and the moths flutter among them as they did in Emily's day. On the top of the moor, the bog – where Cathy loses her shoes – glistens in the sunlight and the wind makes undulating waves in the long grass. The images which make the pages of *Wuthering Heights* come alive are clearly visible here today.

On the moor beyond Stanbury stands Ponden Hall, the home of the Heaton family in the Brontës' time. It has traditionally been associated with Thrushcross Grange. Visitors to Ponden have no difficulty in imagining what the domestic life of the inhabitants must have been like at a time when there was no electricity, no telephone, and the tracks across the moor were rendered impassable by heavy snow or rain.

PRIMITIVE AND HAUNTING

Babbage talks in his report of the 21 per cent of Haworth's dead who received no medical attention in the days before their deaths. For the people living in the isolated farmhouses on upper parts of the moor the percentage was much higher. What hope of a doctor on a winter night if you lived on the top of the moor? Even less chance if you had no money to pay his fees. Babbage himself was worried that, where no cause of death was entered on a certificate because no doctor had seen the dying, there was great opportunity for the committing of crime: "from murder in its naked form, through the various finely shaded gradations of ill-treatment, starvation, and neglect, down to that thoughtless inattention to the requirements of infant life to which the children of the poor are but too frequently exposed."

Such crimes were not necessarily those of the poor alone: we have only to think of how Hindley treated Heathcliff, and of Heathcliff's own treatment of Hareton to realize what possibilities of abuse there were among all classes, particularly in isolated communities. When Linton is dying at Wuthering Heights and Catherine asks Heathcliff to send for the doctor, he replies:

… his life is not worth a farthing, and I won't spend a farthing on him … None here care what becomes of him; if you do, act the nurse; if you do not, lock him up and leave him.

ALCOMDEN STONES, HAWORTH MOOR, WEST YORKSHIRE.

There is no suggestion, of course, that Heathcliff might be held to account for Linton's death. Babbage was obviously right to be worried.

The very isolation, however, of the moors gave them their peculiar primitive and haunting character. For Charlotte, left alone, they were inextricably bound up with the memory of her sisters:

…when I go out there alone everything reminds me of the times when others were with me, and then the moors seem a wilderness, featureless, solitary, saddening. My sister Emily had a particular love for them, and there is not a knoll of heather, not a branch of fern, not a young bilberry leaf, not a fluttering lark or linnet, but reminds me of her. The distant prospects were Anne's delight, and when I look round she is in the blue tints, the pale mists, the waves and shadows of the horizon. In the hill-country silence their poetry comes by lines and stanzas into my mind: once I loved it; now I dare not read it …

THE LAKE DISTRICT

I sent a dose of cooling admonition to the poor girl whose flighty letter reached me at Buckland. It seems she is the eldest daughter of a clergyman, has been expensively educated and is laudably employed as governess in some private family. About the same time that she wrote to me her brother wrote to Wordsworth, who was disgusted with the letter, for it contained gross flattery and plenty of abuse of other poets, including me. I think well of the sister from her second letter, and probably she will think kindly of me as long as she lives.

Branwell was later to write to De Quincey – another unanswered letter – and, during the time he was living in the Lake District as tutor to the Postlethwaite family, he spent what must have been a stimulating day with Coleridge's son, Hartley. It was the nearest he would get to mixing with the famous literary figures he admired. By the time Charlotte went to stay in the area, Southey had been dead for seven years, and she was the well-known writer of *Jane Eyre*.

CHARLOTTE AT AMBLESIDE

WHEN CHARLOTTE WENT to stay in Westmoreland in the summer of 1850, she was visiting an area of England which was, by then, hallowed – the Lake District. Since Wordsworth's return there in 1799, it had been associated with the most important group of writers in the country: Southey, De Quincey and the giants of the Romantic movement, Coleridge and Wordsworth himself. Branwell had written to Wordsworth and Charlotte to Southey in 1837 when they were anxious for encouragement and recognition as young writers. Southey's account of the correspondence and the fact that Wordsworth never replied to Branwell are indications of their dismissive attitudes towards the two unknown correspondents:

Her stay in the Lakes was as the guest of the Kay Shuttleworths, who, on learning the identity of Currer Bell, had already visited Charlotte at the Parsonage. Sir James was an eminent social reformer, who had worked tirelessly for better conditions among the Manchester poor and for improvements in education; he appears to have taken up Charlotte's well-being as another cause worthy of his energy and devotion. Rather against her will, she was persuaded to join them for a week in their holiday house at Ambleside on Lake Windermere; no doubt, the fact that Mrs Gaskell was to be a fellow guest would have proved an attraction to Charlotte.

Her response to the outstanding natural beauty of the Lake District was to want to be alone, just as she was later to indicate to Arthur Bell Nicholls on her honeymoon in the west of Ireland that she needed to commune with nature by herself. He, it appears, was more sensitive to her needs than was Sir James.

Mrs Gaskell records Charlotte's reflections on her first visit to the Lakes:

If I could only have dropped unseen out of the carriage, and gone away by myself in amongst those grand hills and sweet dales, I should have drunk in the full power of this glorious scenery. In company, this can hardly be …

And she wrote, in some impatience, to Miss Wooler:

[Sir James Kay Shuttleworth] very kindly showed me the neighbourhood, <u>as it can be seen from a carriage</u>, and I discerned that the Lake country is a glorious region, of which I had only seen the similitude in dreams, waking or sleeping. Decidedly I find it does not agree with me to prosecute the search of the picturesque in a carriage. A waggon, a spring-cart, even a post-chaise might do; but the carriage upsets everything. I longed to slip out unseen, and to run away by myself in amongst the hills and dales.

The freedom which Charlotte and her siblings had enjoyed, roaming the moors above the Parsonage, enabled her to experience nature very intimately and directly. To see it from a carriage, however magnificent the view, was not to her taste.

Interestingly, and perhaps because of this lack of solitude, there is very little specific record about her reaction to or response to the wonderful Lakeland scenery, although she wrote briefly to her father on arrival at the Kay Shuttleworths', describing the place as "exquisitely beautiful" and the weather as "cloudy, misty, and stormy" with occasional bursts of sunshine, revealing the hills and lake. There is none of the detailed natural description, however, that we might

expect from an admirer of Wordsworth and the writer of *Jane Eyre*. Mrs Gaskell gives us, perhaps, the clearest insight into Charlotte's reaction to nature during their stay, but curiously the landscape is not mentioned at all:

I was struck by Miss Brontë's careful examination of the shape of the clouds and the signs of the heavens, in which she read, as from a book, what the coming weather would be. I told her that I saw she must have a view equal in extent at her own home. She said that I was right, but that the character of the prospect from Haworth was very different; that I had no idea what a companion the sky became to any one living in solitude – more than any inanimate object on earth – more than the moors themselves.

The following winter Charlotte returned to the Lakes to stay with her fellow writer, Harriet Martineau. There, she wrote to Ellen, she enjoyed "the most perfect liberty" afforded to all Harriet's visitors. She does not say whether she was at last able to venture out among the "grand hills and sweet dales" alone.

DOVE COTTAGE, WORDSWORTH'S HOME AT GRASMERE.

VISITS TO FRIENDS

S INCE HER SCHOOLDAYS, Charlotte's two closest friends were Ellen Nussey and Mary Taylor.

THE RYDINGS, BIRSTALL, WEST YORKSHIRE, THE HOME OF ELLEN NUSSEY. THE EXTERIOR OF THE HOUSE, WITH ITS CASTELLATED ROOF, WAS ALMOST CERTAINLY A MODEL FOR THORNFIELD HALL IN "JANE EYRE".

THE NUSSEY HOME

Charlotte's first visit to Ellen's home was in September 1832, when Charlotte was sixteen. Ellen was the youngest daughter of a family of twelve children — a family who had made their money in the local industry of cloth-manufacturing but were no longer as wealthy as they had been. Their house — one of several the family owned — was called The Rydings; with its castellated roof-line, it was to furnish — at least partially and exter- nally — a model for Thornfield Hall in *Jane Eyre*. More

importantly, the whole area was to provide, many years later, the setting for *Shirley*. Only a few miles from Bradford, it was the scene of some of the first industrial developments in the textile trade, although, as Butler Wood comments, "In the early part of last century the mills were sparsely scattered in a smiling landscape."

In this landscape we find Oakwell Hall, the magnifi- cent sixteenth-century manor house that becomes Fieldhead in *Shirley* and The Red House at Gomersal — her fictional Yorke family's home, Briarmains. All the houses are within a few miles of each other and within easy reach both of Roe Head School and Hartshead, where Patrick was curate before moving to Thornton. It is not surprising that Charlotte, having decided to write a more "realistic" novel, should choose to place it in this part of Yorkshire, familiar to her both by family associa- tion and in her own experience.

In later years Charlotte stayed with Ellen at Brookroyd, the house to which the Nussey family moved in 1836. It was while visiting there in 1848 that she cor- rected the proofs of *Jane Eyre*, although she did not actually admit to Ellen that she was the author until after Emily's death. Emily's reluctance to be identified as the writer of *Wuthering Heights* may have been one reason for Charlotte's reticence with Ellen; it is very possible, too, that she did not find it easy to share her creative world with a friend, however close, whose nature was not itself rooted in the imagination.

THE TAYLOR HOME

That Charlotte's visits to the Taylor family at the Red House made a lasting impression on her is clear from her reconstruction of both the house and the family in *Shirley*. Mr Yorke's Whig sympathies are those of Mary and Martha Taylor's father, and their brothers are the models for the Yorke boys. The political discussions and arguments, the strong anti-Tory stance, the lively, aggressive jostling for position in a family are all there. So is the young Martha Taylor, later to die of cholera in Brussels, and the independent, able Mary. On receiving her copy of *Shirley*, when it finally arrived in New Zealand, Mary wrote to Charlotte:

> *You make us all talk much as I think we should have done if we'd ventured to speak at all … There is a strange feeling in reading it of hearing us all talking. I have not seen the matted hall and painted parlour windows so plain these five years … 'Shirley' is much more interesting than 'Jane Eyre', who never interests you at all until! she has something to suffer …*

Reading about oneself, of course, is always interesting!

Mr Taylor, a Nonconformist – in political as well as religious terms – was, like the Nussey family, in the textile trade. Like Mr Yorke in *Shirley*, he spoke fluent French; he was used to trading with the Continent and encouraged Charlotte, of whom he was very fond, in her reading of European literature. The Red House was a cultured place and the Taylor family's interests were much more akin to the Brontës' than were the Nusseys', for whom social position was very important – no doubt the more so since Ellen's father's death and a decline in the family fortunes.

The two houses reinforce the contrast between the Taylors and the Nusseys: The Rydings a large, imposing residence, with its Gothic battlements; The Red House discreet, unpretentious, compact, classical.

For Charlotte both these families, however, represented places where she could feel at home. She was with girls whom she knew intimately and on whose loyalty and support she could depend. They both came from wealthier homes than she did – although both were experiencing financial difficulties in the 1830s – but she brought to her relationships with them a unique

quality which they admired and respected, as their accounts of her show.

OTHER VISITS

After the deaths of her sisters she was invited to spend brief spells with several of her new-found acquaintances and well-wishers, but it is doubtful whether she would have looked on them as real friends, with the possible exception of Smith Williams and, in the last years, of Mrs Gaskell. Among those whose hospitality she was invited to share were George Smith, her publisher, and his mother; the Kay Shuttleworths, with whom she spent time in the Lake District; Harriet Martineau, well-known novelist and journalist, and a supporter of the Whigs and social reform. Much as she appreciated Harriet Martineau's kindness and intellectual company, she was to name her specifically – in a letter to Smith Williams – as one who could never replace Ellen Nussey in her affections.

THE RED HOUSE, GOMERSAL, WEST YORKSHIRE, HOME OF THE TAYLOR FAMILY — BRIARMAINS IN "SHIRLEY".

SCARBOROUGH

SCARBOROUGH, C. 1850.
THE COMING OF THE
RAILWAY HERALDED
FURTHER EXPANSION
OF THE TOWN IN THE
SECOND HALF OF THE
NINETEENTH CENTURY.

THE DISCOVERY, IN THE 1620S, of the Spaw Well by Elizabeth Farrow marked the birth of the spa town where Anne Brontë lies buried. But the town has a much longer history than that of its spa.

Its magnificent site on the cliffs overlooking the North Sea had attracted inhabitants as far back as the Iron Age: they built a fort on the hill there and the Romans a signal station. It was a later visitor who probably gave his name to the town, a Viking invader who settled in Scarborough in 966. His nickname was Skarthi, or "the hare lip". According to the Norse Kormakssaga, "the brothers Thorgils [Skarthi] and Kormak went harrying in Ireland, Wales, England, and Scotland, and ... were the first men to set up the stronghold which is called Scarborough."

Where the Iron Age fort and the Roman signal station stood on the top of the hill, commanding a magnificent view over the sea to the east, the remains of the twelfth-century castle now dominate the town, as they did in Anne Brontë's day. The castle's history has been a turbulent one: it survived numerous sieges from the fourteenth to the seventeenth centuries, until finally being rendered defenceless by Parliamentary forces during the Civil War.

The importance of Scarborough as a harbour was already established by the thirteenth century, when clearly in Scarborough's best interests to build a new port so that all ships could sail in and out of her safely. As might be expected of a seaside town, fishing and shipbuilding have been its main forms of employment and sources of income. Even in the fourteenth century, when larger ports like Hull were expanding their trade with the exporting of wool, Scarborough seems to have relied on its traditional industries.

A FASHIONABLE SPA

By the time Anne Brontë visited Scarborough for the first time, shipbuilding was already declining and the port losing its importance as a trading centre. The use of iron in shipbuilding, rather than wood – of which there was a plentiful local supply – meant that Scarborough was less competitive than other yards. An additional cause of the decline in Scarborough's trade was the difficulty some of the new larger iron ships had entering and leaving the harbour, which was too small to accommodate them. Consequently, the town needed to find other means of attracting income: the further expansion and development of the Spa in the nineteenth century helped meet this need.

Although Elizabeth Farrow discovered her mineral spring in the 1620s and visitors had come to Scarborough to drink the healing water ever since, it was not until the second half of the eighteenth century that the town started to become a fashionable spa resort, "one of the most ancient and respectable bathing places in great Britain", as a 1785 guide to the town describes it. It was at this time that the Georgian expansion of the town began in earnest, with the building of new houses on the cliff. Rooms there, in 1785, could be rented for ten shillings a week.

The first half of the nineteenth century saw further development, including the building of the magnificent terrace where Anne Brontë stayed with the Robinsons on her first visit to Scarborough in the early 1840s. By that time, the Cliff Bridge Company had been formed and had developed the whole Spa area: a new bridge to reach the Spa House and a Gothic saloon.

Arthur Rowntree's description of Scarborough's provision for debtors in its gaol just after the turn of the century suggests there was another Scarborough which the fashionable visitor did not see. It's certainly unlikely that Anne Brontë saw any but the most respectable areas of the town.

Her employers, the Robinson family, spent a number of summer holidays there and always took lodgings in the most fashionable quarter; it would have furnished them with all the social amenities considered necessary for people of their class: during the season there would have been ample opportunity for them to enjoy, and to be seen in, the tea-rooms, at balls and concerts, out walking in the parks and on the cliffside paths. To Anne Brontë, the governess, this fashionable world can have had little appeal. She may well have been glad of the existence of a lending-library, but, most importantly, what Scarborough gave her was her first sight of the sea. Some eight years later, hoping that "change of air or removal to a better climate" might effect a cure for her tuberculosis, she chose to go back there – to die.

In 1845 – between Anne's first and last visits – the railway came to Scarborough. It was a development which was to make further expansion of the town both possible and profitable: the Grand Hotel and large, solid Victorian houses bear witness to the town's prosperity in the second half of the nineteenth century. At the time of Anne's death, however, much of that development lay ahead. The Scarborough she knew and loved is the one recorded in Ellen's description of the day before she died:

The evening closed in with the most glorious sunset ever witnessed. The castle on the cliff stood in proud glory gilded by the rays of the declining sun. The distant ships glittered like burnished gold … The view was grand beyond description. Anne was drawn in her easy chair to the window, to enjoy the scene with us. Her face became illumined almost as much as the scene she gazed upon.

SCARBOROUGH
TODAY, STILL
AN ATTRACTIVE
SEASIDE TOWN.

SCARBOROUGH

BELGIUM

Following the end of the Napoleonic Wars, Belgium and Holland had been united under William of Orange, who had embarked on a number of economic improvements to the country: new roads, a canal joining Ghent to the North Sea, greatly increased coal production, the setting-up of ironworks and glassworks, the establishment of an industrial bank and of a state system of education. Yet, in spite of these material improvements in the country's fortunes, William was unpopular. The Belgians saw him as favouring the Dutch half of the country, in both taxation and parliamentary representation; they also objected very strongly to having a Protestant king ruling over their predominantly Catholic country. So it was that in 1830 Belgium had its own revolution, resulting in her independence.

The country was ideally suited both geographically and politically to take full advantage of any opportunities for economic development, and the decades that followed saw continuing progress. In the 1830s Brussels Free University was founded and the country saw Europe's first passenger train service launched in 1835 in Stephenson's presence. Impressive, wide new streets replaced the rotting slums of the old city, although a government inquiry of 1846 still found appalling poverty and malnutrition among the Belgian poor. During these years of industrial development, there were very close links between England and Belgium, with many English engineers and navvies working alongside their continental colleagues.

BRUSSELS, C.1850, SHORTLY AFTER CHARLOTTE AND EMILY WERE THERE.

WHEN CHARLOTTE AND EMILY arrived in Brussels in February 1842, it was only twenty-seven years after the Battle of Waterloo. They must have been, one imagines, acutely conscious of that battlefield, lying only 20 kilometres to the south of the city – a battlefield where thirty-nine thousand men had died so recently and where Charlotte's hero, Wellington, had lived up to everything she expected of him. All the horror of battle would have lost its immediacy by then, but some people must have remembered the smell of rotting flesh permeating even to the city in the aftermath of the carnage.

The Brontë sisters arrived in Brussels at an important and optimistic time in the country's history. Wellington's defeat of Napoleon had brought peace to Europe, and Belgium's own struggle for independence had resulted, in 1831, in her recognition as an independent state. By 1839, just three years before Charlotte's and Emily's arrival, her independence and neutrality were finally guaranteed by the Treaty of London.

A GRAND
OLD WORLD

It was to this Belgium that Charlotte and Emily came. As Mrs Gaskell says,

> *... there was much in Brussels to strike a responsive chord in her [Charlotte's] powerful imagination. At length she was seeing somewhat of that grand old world of which she had dreamed ... Every spot told an historic tale ... The great solemn Cathedral of St. Gudule, the religious paintings, the striking forms and ceremonies of the Romish Church – all made a deep impression on the girls, fresh from the bare walls and simple worship of Haworth Church.*

Without doubt, the cultural impact of Brussels must have been great. Here were art galleries, concert halls, lecture rooms all on their doorstep, as well as the imposing architecture and grand streets and squares of a thriving European city.

A CLASH OF FAITH

We cannot miss, however, Mrs Gaskell's emphasis on the sisters' reaction to living, for the first time, in a Catholic country. Belgium had not long cast off its Protestant king and was, very probably, more devoutly and adamantly Catholic than she might otherwise have been. It is impossible to read *Villette* without being painfully aware of Charlotte's difficulties with both the native Flemish people and their Catholicism.

In the novel Charlotte expresses forcefully and repeatedly through Lucy Snowe her own anti-Catholic prejudices. Indeed, she links another of her best-loved themes – freedom versus slavery – with the whole question:

> *Each mind was being reared in slavery ... the CHURCH strove to bring up her children robust in body, feeble in soul, fat, ruddy, hale, joyous, ignorant, unthinking, unquestioning ...*

When Lucy goes to confess to a Catholic priest – as Charlotte did when she was in Brussels – she is told: "... our faith alone could heal and help you. Protestantism is altogether too dry, cold, prosaic for you." Beneath all Charlotte's castigations of this Church does there lie a real temptation to succumb to its attraction? Is it altogether too seductive? Certainly, Lucy rejects the priest's suggestion that she come back to see him by saying "As soon should I have thought of walking into a Babylonish furnace."

Lucy is equally scathing of the Belgian pupils at her Brussels school: they are "this wild herd", "this swinish multitude":

> *Severe or continuous mental application they could not, or would not bear: heavy demand on the memory, the reason, the attention, they rejected point-blank.*

Was Charlotte aware of William of Orange's claim that his united parliament gave unfair proportion to Dutchmen because among the Belgian population there were many more illiterates and, therefore, far fewer suitable to hold office? Ironically, she and Emily were to benefit enormously from the education they received there.

ILLUSTRATION TO "VILLETTE", ONE OF CHARLOTTE'S NOVELS, SET IN BRUSSELS.

LONDON

CHARLOTTE AND EMILY first saw London on their way to Brussels in 1842. They stayed then, as Charlotte and Anne were to stay later, at the Chapter Coffee House in Paternoster Row. This was the tavern where Patrick had stayed in his bachelor days during his visits to London as a student at Cambridge and a curate in Essex. Mrs Gaskell describes it as "the resort of all the booksellers and publishers" in the mid-eighteenth century and later as the place where "university men and country clergymen" could catch up on the literary scene. There, in the heart of the City of London, "in the shadow of St. Paul's" and in the very masculine world of the Coffee House, Charlotte was aware of the economic hub of the world. She records her impressions later in the words of Lucy Snowe, who compares it to the West End:

I love the city far better. The city seems so much more in earnest: its business, its rush, its roar, are such serious things, sights, and sounds. The city is getting its living –

the West-end but enjoying its pleasure. At the West-end you may be amused; but in the city you are deeply excited.

If Lucy's experience is Charlotte's, then she felt not only excitement but also a sense of freedom in London:

I went wandering whither chance might lead, in a still ecstasy of freedom and enjoyment; and I got … into the heart of city life. I saw and felt London at last.

By the time she wrote *Villette*, Charlotte had been introduced to the fashionable world of the West End by both George Smith and Smith Williams. When she and Anne went to see her publishers in 1848 to reveal their identities, they were taken to the Opera – where their unsophisticated clothes attracted attention – as well as to an exhibition at the Royal Academy and to the National Gallery.

After Anne's death, Charlotte was to be a fairly frequent visitor to London, as the literary world opened up before her. Writing to Ellen from the city in 1849, she refers to it as "this big Babylon" and speaks of the "whirl" she has been in since arriving to stay with George Smith and his mother: "for changes, scenes, and stimulus, which would be a trifle to others, are much to me." On the same day she wrote to her father of how she had been to see the famous actor Macready in *Macbeth* and to a Turner exhibition; but her most exciting – and moving – moment had been meeting her literary hero Thackeray at dinner the evening before. Six months later she was again staying with the Smiths and had seen some fine paintings at the Royal Academy, "especially a large one by Landseer of the Duke of Wellington on the field of Waterloo, and a grand, wonderful picture of Martin's …" A week later she

saw her hero, the Duke of Wellington, at the Chapel Royal, and visited the House of Commons.

Her visits to London must have meant for Charlotte the physical coming alive of a world she had lived in imaginatively and intellectually since she was a child: the great political figures walked these streets, the pressing political and social issues were debated and decided here. It was in London that she could meet her fellow writers, and here that she could see great art and great plays and hear great music.

The London of the 1840s and 1850s, however, consisted of much more than the political, literary, cultured world which Charlotte saw. Perhaps she had some inkling of the other London when she described the Thames at night as Lucy was rowed to join her ship for Brussels: "Down the sable flood we glided; I thought of the Styx, and of Charon rowing some solitary soul to the Land of Shades." Had she read, one wonders, any of Mayhew's articles published in the London press at the mid-century? Walking the streets of this "Babylon" and in his newspaper office, he had interviewed hundreds, if not thousands, of London's poor: dustmen, coalmen, costermongers, street entertainers, domestic servants, the children exposed to sulphurous gases in the match factories, the small boys who worked for the chimney-sweeps,

the water-cress girls, the "mudlarks". Mayhew's accounts told of unspeakable deprivation and poverty in this wealthy industrial city, the commercial capital of the world. Fifty per cent of children had no formal education at all. Mayhew records talking to one "mudlark", a scavenger for any sellable odds-and-ends on the mudbanks of the Thames at low tide; the boy is nine years old:

It is very cold in winter … to stand in the mud without shoes … He had been one month at school before he went mud-larking … He could neither read nor write … He didn't know what religion his father and mother were, nor did he know what religion meant. God was God, he said. He had heard he was good, but didn't know what good he was to him. He thought he was a Christian, but he didn't know what a Christian was. He had heard of Jesus Christ once, when he went to a Catholic chapel, but he never heard tell of who or what he was, and didn't 'particular care' about knowing … London was England, and England … was in London, but he couldn't tell in what part.

It is not surprising that there was agitation for reform in a society of such contrasts. Both Dickens and Mayhew helped to bring it about simply by making people aware of the conditions in which the poor lived and worked.

4 THE AGE OF THE BRONTËS

THE AGE INTO which the Brontës were born was one of great political and social change. Patrick was born only a year after the signing of the American Declaration of Independence, and, as a boy of twelve in Ireland, he must have been aware of a momentous event taking place on the continent of Europe — the French Revolution. This was to affect the whole development of social and political life far beyond the boundaries of France. Had it not signalled to the Irish that resistance to oppression was possible? The spirit of republicanism, wedded to sheer necessity, was a formidable force behind the Luddites and the Chartists.

The end of the eighteenth and the first half of the nineteenth centuries were dominated by those twin revolutions, the agrarian and the industrial. With the enclosure of land came displacement of many small yeomen farmers. Powerful landowners vied for political and social power with the new class of wealthy industrialists, particularly the rich mill and factory owners of Lancashire and Yorkshire.

For over twenty years, from 1793 to 1815, England was at war with France — a war that became as much a struggle for economic as political supremacy. Napoleon's series of Decrees, which declared a blockade on British exports and ordered the destruction of any British or colonial goods found on the Continent, were very damaging to the country as a whole, but particularly so to the industrially developing North.

The Brontë children were born in the years immediately following the end of the war. Wellington, the great hero of Waterloo and the Treaty of Vienna, became Charlotte's childhood hero, too.

While the end of the war heralded peace in Europe for the next forty years, it did not improve the lot of the ordinary people. Indeed, in many ways their lives were grimmer. The movement of people off the land and into the towns brought with it possible economic advantages, but working conditions in the factories and mills and their general environment were often less attractive than those they had left behind. In addition, there was the dissatisfaction of watching the rich grow richer, while they remained in great poverty.

With increased industrial production and the end of the war there came, of course, more trade and the need for better communications. The building and maintenance of roads improved greatly; but the nineteenth century was dominated by the coming of the railways which revolutionized not only the transport of industrial materials and manufactured goods, but also passenger travel. For the Brontës it meant that they could get to Leeds and Manchester, York, Scarborough and London in much less time and much more comfortably than by road.

Just as in Ireland, oppression, economic necessity and the Famine caused mass emigration, so in the Brontës' England there was continued interest in the New World as a place of freedom and opportunity. Charlotte's friend, Mary Taylor, joined a growing number of those for whom doors would open on the other side of the world.

FROM NAPOLEON TO PALMERSTON

THE NAPOLEONIC WARS marked both the end of one era and the beginning of another. The young Wordsworth had written of the French Revolution:

Bliss was it in that dawn to be alive,
But to be young was very heaven!

By the time he wrote his poem "French Revolution, as it Appeared to Enthusiasts", Wordsworth had changed his views completely, disillusioned by the later excesses of the Revolution and the fact that Britain came to be at war with France for over twenty years.

For many upper- and middle-class Englishmen ideas about the Rights of Man and liberty came to be suspect simply because they had been so vigorously espoused by the revolutionaries, and anything French was to be condemned. Radicals were silenced and imprisoned, their newspapers suppressed, and the Six Acts of 1819 marked the peak of a campaign to stifle public protest.

THE DUKE OF WELLINGTON SATIRIZED IN AN 1827 CARTOON ENTITLED "A WELLINGTON BOOT".

FREEDOM AND PEACE

Slowly, in the aftermath of war, the political grip of reaction began to loosen. In 1824, the notorious Combination Acts were repealed and workmen were free – with some limitations – to form trades unions. The movement slowly grew, reaching its peak in 1834 with Robert Owen's Grand National Consolidated Trades Union. The case of the "Tolpuddle Martyrs" was mainly responsible for its collapse. Public protest and a huge petition finally resulted, in 1836, in a pardon for the six Dorset agricultural workers who had been transported to Australia for administering illegal oaths to fellow members of their union branch. In 1834, however, victory appeared to be on the side of the government and repression.

Another successful campaign was the fight for Catholic emancipation, politically significant mainly in Ireland, where the majority of voters were Catholic. Daniel O'Connell's peaceful and successful plan to organize a mass movement to obtain for Catholics the right to vote and sit in Parliament was won in 1829 in spite of Tory party divisions on the subject. Wellington, who was Prime Minister, foresaw civil war if the reform was rejected and persuaded Peel, in spite of his personal objections, to support it. Patrick Brontë publicly supported Catholic emancipation in letters he wrote to the Tory *Leeds Intelligencer* at this time. We also know, of course, that he opposed the repeal of the Act of Union in the 1840s. In both instances he was on the "winning" side.

Ireland also played a part in the success of the Anti-Corn League's struggle for free trade. English agriculturalists had enjoyed great prosperity during the Napoleonic Wars when only they could supply the food the country needed. Industrialists, on the other hand, wanted to open the ports and send their products all over the world. German states, for example, could only buy English textiles and machinery in exchange for wheat and potatoes. In the 1820s Tory reformers had begun simplifying and relaxing tariffs, and in his second ministry of 1842–6 Peel continued this work. The Corn Laws, however, were still regarded as sacred by the majority of the party, and it was not until 1845 that the Irish Famine made it possible to argue successfully for repeal: the need to provide help for the starving Irish rather than strong economic argument brought about the end of the Corn Laws in 1846.

POLITICAL REFORM

The Reform Act of 1832 marked the beginning of a series of changes in the composition of Parliament and the qualifications for voting – changes culminating only in the twentieth century with the granting of votes for women. The Act abolished a number of "rotten" and "pocket" boroughs, giving large industrial towns like Manchester and Birmingham representation in Parliament for the first time. It introduced a new, more rational franchise which effectively gave middle-class householders the right to vote; but it fell far short of radical demands for a secret ballot and the vote for working men. Nevertheless, the parliament elected under the new system brought in a range of important measures, including the abolition of slavery in the British Empire, the first effective Factory Act for the textile industry, and the first state grant for education. For the business community, penny postage was to prove one of its most beneficial measures: within twenty-five years the number of postal items handled rose from 76 to 642 million.

The most unpopular "reform" was the Poor Law Amendment Act of 1834 which ended a system of allowances that had come in during the Napoleonic

Wars and offered only the workhouse to the old, sick, or unemployed if they could not support themselves. Patrick Brontë joined the many who opposed the Act.

Nearly forty years of peace in Europe ended with the outbreak of the Crimean War in 1854. The series of humiliating defeats suffered by the British army led to the resignation of the Prime Minister, Lord Aberdeen, and the very popular choice of Lord Palmerston as his replacement. He was to oversee a more successful campaign in the Crimea.

It was, however, economic rather than military success that the country enjoyed at the half century. The Great Exhibition of 1851 advertised Britain's claim to be the "workshop of the world" and was immensely popular, both at home and abroad. Charlotte visited it a number of times during a visit to London, writing to her father: "All the other sights seem to give way to the great Exhibition, into which thousands and tens of thousands continue to pour every day ... I almost wonder the Londoners don't tire a little of this vast Vanity Fair."

FATHER MATHEW, WHO WORKED TIRELESSLY TO EASE SUFFERING DURING THE IRISH FAMINE, COMFORTS A STARVING FAMILY.

FROM NAPOLEON TO PALMERSTON

THE LUDDITES

GIBSON MILL,
CALDERDALE, WEST
YORKSHIRE. MILLS
LIKE THIS AND
RAWFOLDS DOMINATED
THE NORTHERN
LANDSCAPE IN
THE BRONTËS' TIME.
MANY OF THEM
SURVIVE TODAY.

As the industrial revolution gathered momentum, the inevitable introduction of machinery into the textile mills meant that jobs were at risk, just as electronic developments in our own day have caused unemployment. For the poor working classes at the beginning of the nineteenth century, unemployment meant terrible hardship, probable starvation. It is in this climate that the Luddites joined together to fight the industrial progress which threatened their livelihoods and their very lives. It was Ned Ludd, the man who led the first rioters in breaking machinery, who gave his name to the movement.

The government of the day, mindful of the success of the republican cause in the French Revolution only twenty years earlier, and still recovering economically from the effects of the long Peninsular War with France, was not in a mood to be sympathetic to these industrial rebels. Far from addressing the economic causes of social unrest, the government resorted to strong-arm tactics and repression. In the absence of a police force to restrain them and enforce order, soldiers were used to put down Luddite resistance to change in the mills.

THE RIOTS OF 1812

Mrs Gaskell gives a vivid, if sometimes inaccurate, account of the Luddite riots of 1812. They took place in an area of Yorkshire which touched on Charlotte's life – near Roe Head, although years before she went there – and only a few miles from the church at Hartshead where Patrick was curate. According to Mrs Gaskell, Miss Wooler entertained her pupils with stories of the riots and,

> … the times when watchers or wakeners in the night heard the distant word of command, and the measured tramp of thousands of sad desperate men receiving a surreptitious military training, in preparation for some great day which they saw in their visions, when right should struggle with might and come off victorious: when the people of England, represented by the workers of Yorkshire, Lancashire, and Nottinghamshire, should make their voice heard in a terrible slogan, since their true and pitiful complaints could find no hearing in Parliament.

The Brontë children would also have heard all about the Luddite riots from Patrick; the violence on his own doorstep had made such an impression on him that, for the rest of his life, he kept a loaded pistol by him at night. The incident which affected Patrick most and was to be remembered in *Shirley* was the storming of Rawfolds Mill in April 1812. The mill belonged to William Cartwright, who had introduced the latest machinery for the dressing of woollen cloth. According to Mrs Gaskell, he was already unpopular among the local people and was regarded with some suspicion on account of his "foreign blood". Aware of the hostility he had aroused and prepared for an attack by the Luddites, he barricaded himself into the mill for the night. Again, Mrs Gaskell's description of the scene is graphic: "On every step of the stairs there was placed a roller, spiked with barbed points all round, so as to impede the ascent of the rioters, if they succeeded in forcing the doors."

Although the rioters outnumbered by hundreds those besieged in the mill – William Cartwright himself, four of his own workmen and five soldiers – they were soon defeated. No doubt, superior arms, a position of strength from which to repress the attack and better filled stomachs all played a part in the success of the millowner and his supporters. In any event, while they remained unscathed, two of the Luddites were killed.

PATRICK'S HUMANITY

Patrick's position was unequivocal in that he abhorred the violence employed by the rioters. It is difficult to imagine, however, a fair-minded clergyman with a social conscience not being distressed by the causes which led to the social unease of the time. From all that we know of Patrick Brontë, it is very likely that his response to the men who were rioting – as opposed to the violence itself – was a humane one. He will have seen, among his own parishioners at Hartshead, the suffering which introduction of new industrial production methods caused, and it seems probable that he shared his daughter's sympathy for the "work-people", whose lot she describes in *Shirley* when talking of her millowner, Robert Moore:

> Not being a native, nor for any length of time a resident of the neighbourhood, he did not sufficiently care when the new inventions threw the old work-people out of employ: he never asked himself where those to whom he no longer paid weekly wages found daily bread; and in this negligence he only resembled thousands besides, on whom the starving poor of Yorkshire seemed to have a closer claim.

WILLIAM HORSFALL, A YORKSHIRE MERCHANT AND MANUFACTURER, IS MURDERED BY LUDDITES NEAR HUDDERSFIELD.

NEWSPAPERS

largely responsible for lowering the cost of production. Literature of all kinds – books, periodicals, newspapers – could be produced more quickly and, because of improved methods of transportation, disseminated much more easily and speedily throughout the country.

At the same time, during the last years of the eighteenth century and the first half of the nineteenth, the press was seen as a potentially dangerous tool for radical expression. Any vehicle which might extend the people's awareness of their wrongs, the possibility of redress or even just the existence of others fighting against injustice and oppression was threatening to a government already worried about social unrest. In addition, the growing literacy of the people during the nineteenth century meant that the press could reach an ever-widening audience.

All these factors led successive governments to reinforce more stringently regulations which had existed for the control of all publications since the seventeenth century. Every periodical classed as a newspaper had to be stamped to show that it had paid a tax for its licence. In 1789, with Revolution raging in France, the newspaper tax was raised to tuppence a sheet, and at the end of the Napoleonic Wars in 1815 the tax doubled to four pence. Fines were high, £20, for those found in possession of an unstamped paper. Under the Blasphemous & Seditious Libels Act of 1819, magistrates and constables could seize all copies of any publication offending against the Act, and anyone found guilty of a second offence was sentenced to transportation.

The result of all these curbs on a free press meant that the majority of middle- and working-class people had no access to a newspaper of any kind. There were,

"THE MONTHLY INTELLIGENCER", A MINIATURE NEWSPAPER PRODUCED BY BRANWELL, 1833.

IT IS NOT SURPRISING THAT, in an age of great industrial and social change, the press should play a very important role, nor that the industrial developments themselves should facilitate that role. Steam-printing, introduced in 1814, was of course, passionate opponents to this tax and others which pushed up the price of papers beyond the reach of all but the wealthier classes. Whigs, Radicals and working-class intellectuals all protested vehemently against the taxes, but it was not until 1861 – six years after the death of Charlotte – that the Association for the Repeal of Taxes on Knowledge and all its supporters finally won their battle, and the last of the taxes – the paper duty – was removed.

COBBETT AND CARLILE

Of those fighting for the freedom of the press in the early part of the nineteenth century, the names of William Cobbett (1763–1835) and Richard Carlile (1790–1843) stand out. Cobbett's *Political Register*, which first appeared in 1802, made outspoken attacks on the government, the Industrial Revolution, and the disgraceful state of London; it also called for Parliamentary Reform. In order to be able to publish the weekly paper legally, Cobbett paid stamp duty on *Political Register*, which made it prohibitively expensive for the majority of the population. Cobbett's next publication, *Twopenny Trash*, was designed as a small magazine in order to exempt it from duty: with sales of fifty thousand a week, however, it represented much too

much of a threat to be allowed to continue – the Publications Act of 1819 introduced measures which meant that it, with others of its kind, was liable to duty, and the paper ceased.

Richard Carlile declared his commitment to the cause in *The Republican*: "My whole and sole object … has been a Free Press and Free Discussion". In that cause was not only he imprisoned but also his wife and sister. That he had amazing and courageous support from many ordinary men is evident from the fact that, while the Carliles were in prison, copies of *The Republican* continued to be sold, in spite of prosecutions against the vendors.

In this climate, provincial newspapers played a major role during the first half of the nineteenth century. The provinces found their voice in the local press: the manufacturers of Leeds and Bradford read not the national papers but such publications as the *Leeds Mercury*, whose founder urged both the abolition of stamp duties and the reform of the libel laws. The forming of the Provincial Newspaper Society in 1837 reflects the social and political importance of these papers – two hundred across the country by 1846. In Yorkshire, there were a number of papers available to the Brontës, among them the *Leeds Mercury*, the *Leeds Intelligencer* (to which Patrick wrote in support of the repeal of the Poor Law Amendment Act), the *Halifax Guardian* and the *Bradford Herald*, in both of which Branwell had poetry published.

In addition to the provincial papers, not only were there the established national newspapers, like *The Times*, *The Morning Chronicle* and *The Morning Herald*, but the first half of the nineteenth century also saw the birth of specialist journals like the *Economist*, the *Educational Times*, the *Musical Times*, the Catholic *Tablet*, and the Chartist *The Northern Star*.

The Industrial Revolution – with its introduction of steam-printing and more efficient means of distribution – together with increased literacy and the determined fight for free expression meant that, by the time of the abolition of taxes on newspapers in the early 1860s, the press, as we know it today, was established.

WILLIAM COBBETT, WHO PLAYED A VERY IMPORTANT ROLE IN THE FIGHT FOR THE FREEDOM OF THE PRESS.

NEWSPAPERS

MONARCHY
AND MORALITY

An old, mad, blind, despised, and dying king, –
Princes, the dregs of their dull race, who flow
Through public scorn, – mud from a muddy spring –
Rulers who neither see, nor feel, nor know,
But leech-like to their fainting country cling …

S O WROTE SHELLEY in his *Sonnet: England in 1819*. Not all contemporaries shared his view of George III (1738–1820) and his family; but very few, if any, respected the monarchy.

BATTLE FOR THE THRONE

George III's frequent bouts of insanity – or porphyria, as medical historians now describe his condition – had long allowed his son, who became Prince Regent in 1811, to play a leading role, not only in society but also in politics. The need to provide an heir to the throne had

led to the Prince marrying Princess Caroline of Brunswick-Wolfenbüttel. The sole child of that marriage, Princess Charlotte, married Prince Leopold of Saxe-Coburg. The couple, young, attractive and popular, raised hopes of a stable succession to the throne – hopes dashed less than a year later, in 1817, when both mother and baby died in childbirth.

Of George III's fifteen children, there were now twelve surviving – five ageing princesses and seven princes. None of them had a child who was not illegitimate or otherwise barred from the succession. The spectacle of three princes – the Dukes of Clarence, Cambridge and Kent – hurrying to the altar in order to provide a legitimate heir was not an edifying one. Marriage had now become attractive: it would mean an increased allowance from Parliament and the possibility of power and influence as the parent of a future king or queen. From the country's point of view, the only successful outcome of these marriages was the birth of Princess Victoria to the Duke and Duchess of Kent.

ROYAL SCANDAL

The married life of the Prince Regent, later George IV (1762–1830), had long been a gift to cartoonists and satirists. In 1795, anxious to secure the succession, he married Princess Caroline, despite the fact that ten years earlier he had contracted an "illegal" – because she was a Roman Catholic – marriage with Mrs Fitzherbert. The marriage to Caroline was a sordid – and public – failure. Although he wanted a divorce, particularly when his father, George III, finally died in 1820, he was opposed by his government, who saw the case bringing

A SATIRICAL CARTOON, ONE OF MANY DEPICTING GEORGE IV AND HIS WIFE, CAROLINE.

the monarchy into disrepute; and the King was forced to accept his married state, although the Queen was living abroad.

There was some public support for Caroline, who became briefly the focus of radical discontent: a wronged brave women, suffering as the majority of the people did, under a government that suppressed their liberties. Her last attempt to embarrass her husband, a month before her death, was to try to attend his coronation as King George IV, but she was prevented from entering the Abbey.

"THE SAILOR KING"

William IV (1765–1837) was the third son of George III and succeeded his brother, George IV, in 1830. He was nicknamed "the sailor king", as he had a career in the navy from a young age, rising to the rank of Lord High Admiral in 1827. Like his brother, his private life caused great scandal: his relationship with the celebrated actress Dora Jordan, with whom he lived for many years, resulted in 10 children. In 1818 he married Adelaide of Saxe–Meiningen. Neither of the couple's daughters survived infancy, resulting in the succession to the throne of William's niece, Victoria.

VICTORIA

After her father died of pneumonia within a year of his marriage, Victoria (1819–1901) was brought up by her mother in Kensington Palace. Her half-sister, Feodora, referred to her time there as "imprisonment" and Victoria herself later described her youth as "rather melancholy". Her life was certainly lonely and restricted, partly because her mother was unpopular with George IV, Victoria's "Uncle King", and partly because the Duchess understandably wanted to keep her daughter away from the corruption and dissipation of court life.

Princess Victoria's accession to the throne in 1837, on the death of her uncle William IV, at first made little difference to life at court. In deference to her youth and sex, the dissipated atmosphere of the earlier years was

much less evident; but there was certainly plenty of entertainment and frivolity. In a period of great social and political change, the role facing the young Queen was a daunting one, and she took as her mentor and friend Lord Melbourne, the Prime Minister: her reliance on him emotionally meant that she soon became much too closely identified with the Whig party.

In 1839 she came into open disagreement with Sir Robert Peel, poised to become Prime Minister, over the political affiliation of all her ladies-in-waiting: she refused to replace any of them with the Tories Peel wanted. Without the Queen's confidence, Peel declined to take office, and the conflict led to the Whig cabinet remaining in power for another two years. Other problems, like her personal hostility to Lady Flora Hastings, also contributed to a decline in her popularity after her first year as queen. It was to be her marriage to Prince Albert of Saxe-Coburg-Gotha that brought emotional fulfilment to Victoria and stability both to her personally and the monarchy.

With Victoria's marriage to Albert in 1840, the atmosphere at court slowly began to change. By 1842, Lady Lyttleton was noting that at dinner, instead of gossip, there were serious discussions of naval and scientific subjects. The birth of nine children to the Queen inevitably made the Royal Family – rather then Victoria alone – the focus of attention. Prince Albert's introduction of German customs like the Christmas tree were widely accepted and adopted, and the Queen's example in church-going, charity and her courage in the face of numerous assassination attempts were expressions of a moral code far in advance of her uncles'.

The monarchy came to reflect and inspire the middle-class values which led to the term "Victorian" becoming a synonym for respectability, church attendance and family life. Neither the aristocracy – who continued to enjoy such pastimes as gaming and secret love affairs much as they had in Regency England – nor the working class – who frequently neglected to register their "marriages" – had much sympathy with the "reformed" monarchy. Nevertheless, for most of Queen Victoria's reign it was no longer inappropriate to use the terms "monarchy" and "morality" in the same breath.

VICTORIA, WHO CAME TO THE THRONE AT THE AGE OF 18 AND REIGNED FOR NEARLY 64 YEARS.

CHURCH
AND CLERGY

CHARLES WESLEY
(1707–88) WHO, WITH
HIS BROTHER, JOHN
(1703–91), FOUNDED
THE METHODIST
MOVEMENT.

W E TEND TO THINK of the nineteenth century as a very religious period
in English history – the period which
produced most of our hymns, built those large Gothic
churches scattered across England in the bigger industrial
towns, and the period in which everybody went to
church. It comes as something of a surprise to us, therefore – and a shock to Victorian contemporaries – to
learn that in 1851 a religious census revealed only just
over seven million people attending church out of a pop-

ulation of nearly eighteen million. To those clergy working among the poor, however, it will not have been quite
so surprising.

"A PIECE OF PATRONAGE"

When Jane Austen portrayed Mr Collins in *Pride and
Prejudice* as concerned only about pleasing his patron,
Lady Catherine de Bourgh, she was satirizing a type of
clergyman all too common in the eighteenth century
and the first half of the nineteenth. Anne Brontë contrasts her "good" Mr Weston with the worldly rector, Mr
Hatfield, in *Agnes Grey*. Agnes is "decidedly pleased
with the evangelical truth of his [Mr Weston's] doctrine,
as well as the earnest simplicity of his manner, and the
clearness and force of his style." In contrast, when
speaking of Mr Hatfield, she says it is

> somewhat derogatory to his dignity as a clergyman to
> come flying from the pulpit in such eager haste to shake
> hands with the squire, and hand his wife and daughters
> into their carriage, and, moreover, I owe him a grudge for
> nearly shutting me out of it.

Thirty-four years separated the publications of *Pride and
Prejudice* and *Agnes Grey* – in fact, the time gap
between them is much wider since Jane Austen's novel
was originally written in the 1790s – but Mr Collins and
Mr Hatfield are, effectively, brothers.

They highlight a real problem in the Church of
England at that time. The clergy of the established
Church, often the younger sons of the squirearchy or
nobility, too often looked on their livings as "a piece of

patronage". They mixed socially with the local gentry, addressed their sermons – often read – to them, and were, in many cases, quite out of touch with the poor and needy in their parishes. Nancy, in *Agnes Grey*, sums up the neglect they felt:

> [I] began a talking to th' Rector again ... I hardly could fashion to take such a liberty, but I thought when my soul was at stake, I shouldn't stick at a trifle. But he said he hadn't time to attend to me then.

DISSENTERS AND EVANGELICALS

It was in this context that the Methodist and other dissenting churches began to flourish in the second half of the eighteenth century and the beginning of the nineteenth. With their emphasis on good works, on personal faith, and without the stigma of upper-class exclusivity, dissenting Protestant clergy appealed to their working-class congregations in a way that many of the Church of England clergy did not.

There was, then and throughout the nineteenth century, a real attempt by many of the Church of England clergy to put their house in order. This was particularly true in the Evangelical wing of the Church, to which Patrick Brontë belonged. Like others of his persuasion, he became passionately involved in social causes that would better the lot of the poor. In 1837, shocked by the effect of the Poor Law Amendment Act of 1834 on the textile-workers of his own neighbourhood, he addressed a public meeting in Haworth, urging the government to repeal the Act. He was also a driving force in improving education in the area and in fighting for a healthier and more efficient water supply to the town.

It is interesting to see the expansion of the dissenting churches and the Evangelical branch of the Anglican Church in relation to what was happening politically, socially and culturally at the end of the eighteenth and

beginning of the nineteenth centuries. Just as the whole Romantic movement was marked by emphasis on the individual, personal freedom, the expression of emotion, there were parallel developments in religious worship. The singing of Psalms gave way to those fervent, often sentimental, hymns to be found in Victorian hymn books; sermons were more likely to be delivered with passion and conviction and to appeal to the emotions of their hearers. Personal salvation and personal damnation were absorbing topics for believers in the nineteenth century; Anne Brontë was particularly preoccupied and troubled by the issue.

THE OXFORD MOVEMENT

It was predictable, of course, that there would be a reaction to the Protestant Dissenters and the Evangelicals; and it came with the Oxford Movement. It was an attempt by various Anglicans – most notably Newman, Pusey and Keble – to restate the Catholic nature of the Church of England: in 1841 Newman published Tract XC, in which he stated and sought to establish the compatibility of the Anglican Prayer Book's Thirty-Nine Articles with Catholic theology. Charlotte Brontë was twenty-five at the time; the opening pages of *Shirley*, published in 1849, show she was well aware of the Anglo-Catholic movement:

> The present successors of the apostles, disciples of Dr. Pusey and tools of the Propaganda, were at that time being hatched under cradle-blankets, or undergoing regeneration by nursery-baptism in wash-hand-basins. You could not have guessed by looking at any of them that the Italian-ironed double frills of its net cap surrounded the brows of a pre-ordained, specially sanctified successor of St. Paul, St. Peter, or St. John.

The ironical tone makes it quite clear that the Oxford Movement met with scant sympathy in Haworth Parsonage!

CARTOON OF EDWARD BOUVERIE PUSEY (1800–82), ONE OF THE FOUNDERS OF THE OXFORD MOVEMENT.

"THE LORD'S PRAYER", PAINTED ON A PRAYER BOARD THAT ONCE HUNG IN HAWORTH CHURCH.

EDUCATION

PLAQUE TO
COMMEMORATE
THE SCHOOL AT
HAWORTH WHERE
CHARLOTTE ONCE
TAUGHT.

I T WAS NOT UNTIL 1870 that the government began to ensure there were enough schools to accommodate all children between the ages of five and ten. But long before that date two forces had begun to tackle working-class illiteracy – the churches and the radicals.

It was Hannah More and Robert Raikes who pioneered the setting up of Sunday schools, a movement actively supported by Patrick Brontë. Their chief aim was to enable children to read the Bible themselves and to instruct them in religion. This was done on Sundays, the only day when the children were free from their weekday jobs. No wonder attendance was not always high and many children grew up having spent very little time at school. That as many attended as did, however, reflects the hunger for education which many working-class people felt at this time.

The radical movement had a strong tradition of linking politics and education. Hampden Clubs opened Reading Rooms, where those who were not able to read themselves could listen to radical newspapers read aloud. There was a huge radical press: at its peak Cobbett's *Political Register* sold 60,000 copies, and we can be sure that each copy passed through many hands. There was even an alphabet for the children of female reformers: B stood for Bishop, Bible and bigotry; W for Whig, weakness and wicked.

For those parents willing and able to spend a few pence a week, there was quite a choice of schools, at least in the larger towns. They might choose a "dame" or

CHARLOTTE BRONTË (1816-1855) TAUGHT AT THIS SCHOOL BUILT IN 1832 AND RESTORED BY THE CHURCH IN 1966 WITH HELP FROM THE BRONTË SOCIETY.

"common day school", where a woman or man would teach a small group of children, usually in his or her own house. What was taught would depend entirely on the teacher: some might offer reading, writing, "ciphering" and knitting; others might teach book-keeping and other commercial subjects. What they did not teach was religion. This was left to the various church schools.

Schools run by the National Society, founded in 1811, taught Church of England doctrine; those run by the British and Foreign School society, established three years later, were committed to a broad Christian syllabus, acceptable to all the Protestant dissenting churches. In both kinds of school, religion took priority over other subjects and costs were kept down by the use of "monitors", older children who taught the younger ones in small groups. By the age of ten, most children were considered old enough to be at work, helping to support the family with their earnings, however meagre. After 1833, the numbers of church schools increased as state grants were made available for building new schools; Haworth's own new National School was officially opened in 1844 – the fees were two pence a week.

GRAMMAR AND PUBLIC SCHOOLS

Middle-class boys could attend one of the old grammar schools, many of them ancient foundations, dating from Tudor times. Such schools concentrated on the classics,

so were not much use to the sons of the new industrial class whose future lay in business. Mounting pressure for an education offering science and modern languages led to a number of proprietary schools being set up: Cheltenham, Marlborough, Radley and the Leys all started about this time and, free from the constraints of tradition, were able to respond actively to parental demands for a more modern approach.

At the top end of the educational scale came the nine great public schools, including Eton, Winchester and Rugby. When the century began, these schools were at a very low ebb, both academically and morally, and maintaining discipline was a major problem. Woodward records how a "rebellion" among Winchester pupils in 1818 had to be suppressed by soldiers with fixed bayonets. *Tom Brown's Schooldays* gives a vivid picture of the kind of bullying that was commonplace in the public schools; but it also depicts the reforming work of Dr Arnold as the headmaster of Rugby from 1828 to 1842. Compulsory sport, a successful prefect system and the central role of the school chapel were all introduced by Arnold at this time; widely acclaimed, they were soon adopted in other public schools.

The introduction of modern subjects met with much greater resistance and led to the Earl of Gloucester arguing in 1861 that, educationally speaking, the upper classes were "in a state of inferiority to the middle and

lower". It was the same story with the two oldest universities, Oxford and Cambridge. They were dominated by corruption, slackness and privilege and resisted change even more fiercely than the public schools. It was left to the new universities being founded in London and the provinces to respond to the call for a more modern and relevant education.

EDUCATION FOR GIRLS

What did education offer for girls in the first half of the nineteenth century? Those of the working class joined their brothers at "dame" or "church" schools, but they were much more likely to be kept at home to help when domestic crises occurred. Most middle-class girls studied at home with their mothers or governesses, although some – like the Brontë sisters – went away to school. According to the 1851 census, there were nearly twenty-five thousand "ladies" registered as governesses; most of them would have been to school for a year or two in their teens to be "finished" or prepared for marriage.

Not until the mid-century were the first real secondary schools for girls founded – the Queen's College, the North London Collegiate School and Cheltenham Ladies College. University education and the opening up of a wide range of occupations for women still lay in the future.

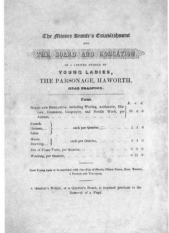

ADVERTISEMENT
FOR "THE
MISSES BRONTË'S
ESTABLISHMENT".
NO PUPILS APPLIED
TO BE TAUGHT AT
THE PARSONAGE.

EDUCATION

COLONIES AND MISSIONARIES

THE AGE OF THE BRONTËS

THE SUCCESSFUL REVOLT of the American colonies at the end of the eighteenth century marked a very important change in British attitudes to the Empire. Many recognized that, as colonies grew larger, more self-sufficient and powerful, they would demand the independence the Americans had sought and won; some, like the philosopher and social reformer Jeremy Bentham, thought they should be encouraged in this aim, particularly as they were, for the most part, an economic burden on Britain rather than an asset.

After 1815 the country was adapting to all the changes and difficulties associated with the coming of peace after a long war. There were war debts to be paid and the whole issue of free trade to be resolved.

Industrialists objected to the preferential position of the colonies and saw them as hindering economic development and Britain's prosperity.

At the same time there were those, like the younger Pitt and his colleagues and disciples, who resisted the threatened disappearance of the British Empire; they wanted to rebuild it on firmer and more liberal foundations. For this to be possible, it would be necessary to construct a new commercial system, and Britain had to face the fact that far-flung colonies were not prepared to be ruled directly from London, nor were they going to pay taxes to Britain.

THE SLAVE TRADE

Aside from the pressing economic problems associated with the colonies, there was one major moral preoccupation for Britain in the early years of the nineteenth century: the slave-trade and slave labour. By 1820 most western European countries had agreed to stop the trade, but there were still 670,000 slaves in the British West Indies. To the reformers, particularly the Evangelicals, this was intolerable. Throughout the colonies, missionaries played a major part not only in resisting the worst atrocities and supporting the victims of oppression, but also in keeping their societies and churches at home informed about conditions where they were working. While they were not, on the whole, either tolerant or broad-minded, most of them brought to their missionary work a spiritual and moral commitment which meant that the welfare of the "natives" was paramount – a welcome contrast with the attitudes of the average settler or landowner.

"THE SLAVEDECK OF THE ALBAROZ", BY DANIEL HENRY MEYNELL, A NINETEENTH CENTURY PAINTING DEPICTING THE HORRIFIC CONDITIONS ON BOARD A SLAVE SHIP.

As a result of increasing outrage among reformers, the Anti-Slave Society was founded in 1823 – William Wilberforce was one of its vice-presidents – and in 1833 an Act was passed which would give freedom to all slaves within a year. It is not surprising that Charlotte Brontë, growing up during these years when slavery was such a moral and political issue, uses the contrasting images and themes of slavery and freedom throughout her novels.

In 1830 Gibbon Wakefield founded the Colonization Society in an attempt to make colonization more systematic. He suggested that emigrants should be from a cross-section of British society rather than recruited solely from among the poor, unemployed or the criminal. He also addressed the question of how land should be allocated to emigrants in order to avoid the problem of vast acres being appropriated by settlers who did not have sufficient labour to work it. His solution was that land should be made more expensive and settlers forced to work for another settler for five years before being allowed to buy their own land. The money raised from the sale of the land should be used to finance emigration of the right kind and class of people. The settlements at Otago and Canterbury in New Zealand, founded in 1848 and 1851 by the Scottish Presbyterian Church and the Church of England respectively, showed that it was possible to finance and organize successful settlements based on the Wakefield model.

INDEPENDENCE

The first half of the nineteenth century saw considerable problems in Canada, with friction particularly between Upper and Lower Canada, which was predominately French. It was feared for a time that Canada would follow the American colonies on the road to independence, but her position within the Empire was assured by the second half of the century. The granting of responsible government to the colony, the question of defence following the American Civil War, and various compromises were enough to reassure her. The South African Cape Colony faced many of the same problems as Canada at this time.

Just as slavery disturbed the British public, so did the transportation to the colonies of criminals, many of them for very petty crimes. In the first half of the century, the number of free immigrants to Australia rose rapidly, and by 1855 transportation had been abolished everywhere but in Western Australia. The attraction of sheep-farming and the discovery of gold encouraged many immigrants, including a number of Chartists who added their voices to the call for more independence from Britain. Aware of Canada's success, Australia pressed for and won responsible government by the mid-1850s.

India – that highly complex society – was to wait some time for self-government. It was to India, of course, that the fictional St John Rivers was preparing to go as a missionary, and of whom Jane Eyre says, "he anticipated his sure reward, his incorruptible crown." She has no doubt that his service in the mission field will have won him that reward, that crown. In the very country to which St John took the Gospel message, many Indians, however, understandably resented his kind of work as an attack on their own Hindu beliefs and customs. In spite of considerable progress towards the granting of political self-determination to many of the larger colonies in the first half of the nineteenth century, it was generally considered that spiritual truth still lay firmly in the hands of the Christian missionary societies and the church.

THE NATIVE CHURCH AT OTAKI IN NEW ZEALAND, C.1851.

COLONIES AND MISSIONARIES

INDUSTRY

was on the market and already installed in a number of textile mills. The introduction of mechanization into the mills and factories heralded a completely new era in textile manufacturing and one which threatened the livelihoods of the men, women and children already working there.

Dreadful as the conditions in the factories were, employment meant the difference between a place to live and food to eat, and homelessness and possible starvation. It was this stark reality which motivated those who, like the Luddites, opposed with violence the introduction of machinery into the mills. For those still employed there the best conditions were to be found in the large purpose-built factories in the towns; but not even in these were there any enforceable conditions of employment.

REFORM

It was only gradually, by a series of Factory Acts throughout the nineteenth century, that the lives of workers were made more tolerable. In the years when the Brontë children were growing up at the Parsonage and writing their stories about Angria and Gondal, factory children were still working from sunrise to sunset for pitiful wages. During the first part of the century, there had been isolated voices, such as Robert Owen's, calling for the protection of children; but the 1819 Factory Act still allowed the employment of any child over the age of nine, and the working day was twelve hours long, exclusive of time taken for meals. It was not until the Reform Bill of 1832 that even the Factory Acts passed were effectually enforced.

"THE DINNER HOUR, WIGAN", BY EYRE CROWE, 1874.

THE "DARK SATANIC MILLS" of Blake's *Jerusalem* still stand today as a monument to Britain's great industrial past, and nowhere are they more evident than in Lancashire and West Yorkshire, even in Haworth itself.

The tremendous changes in the manufacturing industries, which took place at the end of the eighteenth and beginning of the nineteenth centuries, were made possible by developments in industrial methods and machinery. These started with inventions used in cotton-spinning, and spread to the manufacturing of other textiles. With industrial expansion came the need for new sources of power and communications, and by the end of the eighteenth century Watt's steam-engine

In addition to the factory workers, there were those employed in the textile cottage-industries. These workers were divided into those who marketed their own goods and those who worked for an employer who supplied them with raw materials. Many of Mr Brontë's parishioners in Haworth were in this category, working in cramped and poorly ventilated houses. In some of the larger towns, like Manchester and Liverpool, many people involved in this cottage-industry both lived and worked in cellars in appalling conditions.

FLOURISHING INDUSTRIES

The textile industry – so important to the Nottinghamshire, Lancashire and Yorkshire area – was not, of course, the only industry of significance at the beginning of the nineteenth century. With the increased use of the steam-engine came also the development of coal-mining; it was the age of great changes in the production of iron and steel; shipbuilding took on a new importance after the war with France: lost ships had to be replaced and new ones built to cope with expansion in overseas trade.

One of the major industries to flourish as a result of the Industrial Revolution was building. No visitor to Brontë country can miss the great mills to be found in every town or standing stark and forbidding in the valleys; but equally striking are the terraces of millworkers' houses, often built back-to-back, with little or no yard or garden. Most of them are dark, unimaginative dwelling-places, erected quickly and cheaply to house an oppressed and leisure-free workforce. That a more philanthropic and humane attitude could and did prevail among a few employers is evident in the model town, Saltaire in Yorkshire.

There is evidence there, too, as in many of the towns and cities of the North, of the grand municipal buildings which accompanied the wealth of the Industrial Revolution. Classical – and Gothic – libraries, town halls and churches all bear witness to a confident, materialistically successful society. The contrast between the rich and poor is clearly conveyed in nineteenth century architecture.

To enable industry to expand it was necessary to improve channels of communication. Raw materials and manufactured goods had to be transported around a country where, traditionally, the roads had been appallingly inadequate, even for passenger travel. It was not until the early days of the nineteenth century that road-building improved significantly; by this time, the canals were well established and playing a very important part in the transport of industrial goods. Cheaper and safer than road transport, the canals of the North – the Mersey–Trent Canal, the Leeds and Liverpool Canal – flourished until they were superseded by the railways, with whom they were in bitter competition.

It was to be the railway, that revolutionizing product of industrialization, that symbolized, in many ways, the amazing expansion of people's horizons in the nineteenth century.

"BRADFORD, 1825–33", BY JOHN WILSON ANDERSON.

TRANSPORT
AND TRAVEL

THE MANCHESTER
SHIP CANAL.

Transport and travel were revolutionized during the lifetime of the Brontës by the coming of the railways; but it was only in the last years of their lives that they were able to enjoy the freedom and the relative comfort which rail travel brought. For most of their lives they were dependent, like everyone else, on the roads.

ROADS AND CANALS

Until the last years of the eighteenth century and into the first decades of the nineteenth, even travel by road was a hazardous and rather unpredictable business. It was not until the building of the turnpikes and the advent of Telford and Macadam that scientific road-building became widespread throughout the country. The young Brontës lived through the years when coaching was in its heyday, with over three thousand coaches on Britain's roads. For those without the wealth to own a private coach, there were public ones, drawn by four horses and travelling at an average of ten miles an hour.

In addition to the roads, there were also, of course, the canals, constructed as a direct result of the Industrial Revolution. The transporting of coal by road to the big northern cities proved a very slow and difficult task, and the weights carried were particularly damaging to the roads. The Duke of Bridgewater and his engineer, James Brindley, were largely responsible for financing and building the new waterways that carried the coal and other industrial materials between the commercial centres. By 1772 the Manchester–Liverpool Canal was also the main means of passenger travel between the two cities, but not for long. As soon as there were improvements to road-building and the speed of coach travel increased, the canals lost their appeal to passengers. Both forms of travel were threatened, of course, by the 1830s when the possibility of a nationwide rail network became a reality.

THE RAILWAY

The development of rail travel was inevitable long before it actually happened, although it is easier to see that with the benefit of hindsight. Even though locomotives were used in the mines to transport coal as early as 1802, there were those – like the Duke of Wellington – who did not think that passenger trains would come into "extensive use". In 1829, however, Stephenson's Rocket won £500 for the best designed locomotive, and the following year the Manchester–Liverpool line was opened in Wellington's presence. By a tragic irony the event was marred by the death of Huskisson, a former minister, who was fatally injured when he stepped in front of a train; but the Rocket had established its supremacy as a means of travel by reaching the incredible speed of 36 miles an hour.

There were, of course, many people who opposed the new companies springing up across the country to develop this new means of communication. There were those with vested commercial interests, like the canal owners and the Turnpike Trustees. Those who depended on coaching travel, like the inns, the village shops, the horse-owners, all saw their livelihoods threatened by this new steam giant, just as the Luddites had been by the factory machines. Then there were the landed gentry who did not want the railway to come within sight of their estates lest it spoil the view or the trains scare the foxes necessary for the hunt. Before approval could be given for the development of the Great Western line, Eton insisted there should be railway staff appointed to stop boys from using the train during the school term, and Oxford University would not let the railway come nearer than Didcot; when the line was later extended to Oxford, the authorities reserved the right to arrest any student foolish enough to venture onto the station.

In spite of this opposition and the expense which delays involved, private capital continued to be invested in the railways, and by 1848 over 5,000 miles of track were in use. If the railways caused unemployment in some areas, they also provided jobs for thousands: in the laying of tracks, in the building of locomotives and passenger and freight coaches, in the constructing of bridges, tunnels, viaducts and stations. The British "navvy" became a familiar and respected figure, playing his part, too, on the continent, as railways were con-

structed there. By 1843 it was possible to travel by various rail and sea routes to Paris in under forty hours and for a cost of between three and four pounds.

As a result of the expansion of the railways, travel was available to a much wider section of the population. Since the wars with France particularly, the horizons of the British public had been extended – the battlefield of Waterloo, for instance, was a tourist attraction. The upper classes did the Grand Tour and the Romantic poets sought inspiration – and a degree of intellectual and personal freedom – in Italy and beyond. What the railways did was extend the possibility of holidays – however brief – to all but the poorest in society. In 1845 Thomas Cook organized his first excursion, a development which opened up a whole new kind of travel. An excursion ticket from Bradford and Leeds to the Great Exhibition in London cost five shillings. There were even "moonlight trips" to Scarborough from big industrial cities of the North.

The romantic picture of the Brontës isolated in their remote moorland town does not always take account of their very real awareness of the industrial developments taking place around them. For the Brontë sisters the coming of the railway meant much easier access to York, to Scarborough, to London; Charlotte, of course, would go further afield in the last years of her life. Branwell earned a living from the new industry for a time, and Aunt Branwell invested most of her money in York and North Midland Railway shares: they formed the bulk of the sisters' inheritance at her death.

THE LIVERPOOL–
MANCHESTER RAILWAY,
C.1831.

THE POSITION OF WOMEN

FLAX HECKLERS IN
A LEEDS MILL,
C.1846.

F OR MANY WOMEN the first half of the nineteenth century was not a good time to live. In earlier centuries women of all classes had enjoyed active and productive lives. Girls of the upper classes had often been as well educated as their brothers until marriage and motherhood claimed them. Renaissance England boasted many brilliant and scholarly women like Queen Elizabeth and Lady Jane Grey. In their husbands' absence at war or the court, such women ably administered huge estates or even, during the Civil War, defended their homes against attack. Middle-class women worked in their husbands' businesses, sometimes continuing to manage them after they were widowed, and in peasant families work was shared out among all the members, men and women alike.

With the coming of the Industrial Revolution, this began to change. For upper-class women things were not very different: families where women were traditionally highly educated continued to employ tutors and governesses to teach their daughters at home, and even on marriage these daughters enjoyed the protection of their dowries by means of settlements.

Middle-class families, however, began to copy what they saw as the way of life of their social superiors. They took pride in having a wife and daughters untrained in domestic skills – such ignorance showed the family could afford to employ servants. In *Pride and Prejudice*, when Mr Collins tries to ingratiate himself with the Bennet family by asking, after dinner, "to which of his fair cousins the excellence of its cookery was owing", Mrs Bennet "assured him, with some asperity, that they were very well able to keep a good cook, and that her daughters had nothing to do in the kitchen." Earlier generations of middle-class women would have been astonished by this remark. They took pride in being able to cook, brew, preserve food, spin, weave, and do all household tasks – partly for the satisfaction which the exercise of such skills gave them and partly because their knowledge and experience would enable them to detect inefficient services in their households.

The result of such attitudes as Mrs Bennet's was that middle-class girls had very little to occupy their time or their minds. Certainly, girls with access to a good library might read widely, but they often lacked the self-discipline to study systematically and, above all, they lacked recognition that women had a right to intellectual studies. Florence Nightingale, in her essay *Cassandra*, comments bitterly: "Women are never supposed to have any occupation of sufficient importance *not* to be interrupted, except 'suckling their fools'; and women themselves have accepted this …" The common justification of this state of affairs was that serious education was wasted on those who would spend their lives looking after a husband and family; yet, during this period, around half a million "surplus" women never married. How ironic to be prepared, however inadequately, for a career one might never take up!

The only socially acceptable occupations for middle-class women who had to support themselves were dressmaking and teaching or working as governesses. Having been so poorly educated themselves, they could usually only offer a smattering of "accomplishments" – piano-playing, deportment, French, singing, needlework. To remedy this position the Queen's College was opened in 1848, and from then on more opportunities for a solid education became available. This was too late for the Brontë sisters; but all three enjoyed at Roe Head a rather better education than did most girls of the time; and their stay in Brussels introduced Charlotte and Emily to an academic discipline of which they took full advantage, as Monsieur Heger testifies.

For those – the majority of women – who found a husband, the law offered little protection. All a woman's property – unless protected by settlement – became her husband's on marriage. She had no rights over her children, or even who visited her house; should she leave an intolerable marriage, her husband could take any of her earnings, although he owed her no duty of maintenance. Caroline Norton fought and won a partial concession for separated wives in the 1838 Infant Custody Bill, which allowed a separated woman access to her children provided her character was unblemished. But for divorce, women had to wait until 1857, and even then the cost ruled out the process for all but those who had access to wealth.

What of working-class women? Their lives had always been hard, combining housework and childcare with their work on the farms or in the workshops. Now, however, with the collapse of hand industries and threat of the Poor Law, they were driven into the factories and mines and forced to send their children there as well. The 1842 report on conditions in the mines caused public revulsion and a demand for change – not just because of the evidence given about the heavy demands made on women, but because illustrations to the report showed how little clothing men and women wore underground in the intense heat. Even before the Mines Act which followed the report, a beginning had been made to regulate the textile industry where women employees formed the majority. As one working man put it to the Commissioners: how would Prince Albert like it if Queen Victoria wasn't available to make his tea!

It is a reflection on the lack of balance in society at this period that middle-class women suffered severely from a lack of occupation, while working-class women in the industrial areas toiled twelve or more hours a day and carried the additional burden of all their domestic duties.

HELEN GRAHAM, THE GIFTED HEROINE OF "THE TENANT OF WILDFELL HALL", WHO IS TRAPPED IN A HELLISH MARRIAGE.

AN ACCOMPLISHED VICTORIAN GIRL.

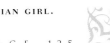

MEDICINE AND SANITATION

IN THE EARLY NINETEENTH CENTURY the general tendency was for the death rate to fall. Bubonic plague had disappeared and smallpox was declining with the efforts in vaccination; but the general lowering of the death rate masked huge local differences. In the 1820s mortality in country districts was estimated to be 18.2 per thousand, compared with 26.2 in the towns. Even more graphically, a table published in 1843 giving the average age at death for three social groups showed how much country life benefited even the poor, compared with the financially better off in the towns:

	MANCHESTER	RUTLAND
Professional, business	38	52
Traders, farmers	20	41
Mechanics, labourers	17	38

"THE LAST OF THE LINE", A SENTIMENTAL VICTORIAN DRAWING OF A DEATHBED SCENE.

THE BABBAGE REPORT ON HAWORTH, 1850.

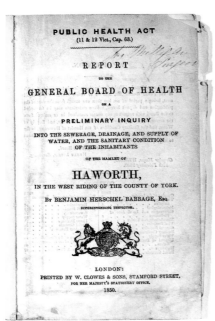

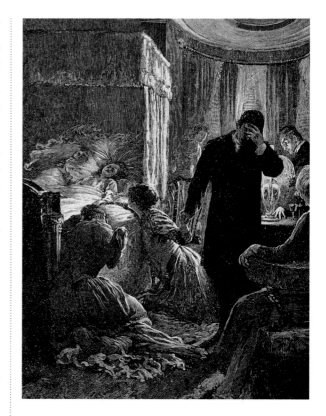

The villain of the piece was the great increase in population, mainly caused by migration to the big towns. Between 1801 and 1831 Manchester, Glasgow and Leeds all doubled their populations without there being any appropriate expansion of housing or improved sanitation. Where extra houses were built they tended to be squeezed into what had been courtyards and passages, so the free flow of air was blocked, and rubbish, both liquid and solid, was often allowed to accumulate. Where sewers existed to carry off rain water, they were overloaded by being connected to house drains, not their original function.

DISEASE AND DEATH

The three main killers at this time were cholera, typhus and tuberculosis. Of these, cholera was the most feared. It was new, the first epidemic striking in 1831, and it killed rapidly on a massive scale, attacking people of all social classes. Once its cause – contaminated water – was recognized, it could be avoided; but it took a long struggle, as the inhabitants of Haworth knew to their cost, to persuade local authorities that clean water would be cheaper in the long run. Mrs Gaskell wrote of "the weary, hard-worked housewives having to carry every bucketful, from a distance of several hundred yards, up a steep street" and described Haworth as "built with utter disregard of all sanitary conditions; the great old churchyard lies above all the houses, and it is terrible to think how the very water-springs of the pumps must be poisoned." One of the last great national cholera epidemics, in 1853, affected Newcastle most severely: its council had refused to use its powers to bring in health reforms.

Typhus was a disease of the slums. Sometimes called "jail fever", it was found on board ship, in prisons and wherever people were packed together in overcrowded and insanitary conditions. Poor food and overwork made people more susceptible to it, so it was treated as a less urgent problem than cholera, which struck the rich as well as the poor.

The third great killer of the nineteenth and first part of the twentieth century was tuberculosis. Often misdiagnosed, it probably accounted for a third of all deaths. Taken for granted as an inevitable part of life, it also reflected overcrowded conditions and an inadequate diet, although there appears to have been an element of hereditary susceptibility to it as well. It is a disease that was virtually eliminated in Britain after the 1950s, but the 1990s have seen an increased incidence of it among the homeless and the least well off in society.

In the first half of the nineteenth century the main obstacle to better sanitation was the cost and the reluctance of the wealthier members of society to spend sufficient money to put right the appalling conditions in which so many lived. Edwin Chadwick, mentioned by Babbage in his 1850 report on Haworth to the Board of Health, worked tirelessly to convince the middle-class ratepayers that the cost of failing to bring in clean water and proper sewage systems would be much greater than the expense of providing these improvements. He cited the burden on the Poor Law and the prisons, as

well as the social and moral cost of overcrowded housing.

It was medical men, Doctors Arnott, Kay and Southwood Smith, who provided Chadwick with the proof he needed to link insanitary conditions and disease. Although he met with a lot of opposition, not helped by his own rather difficult character, Chadwick unearthed the facts and drew the conclusions that were eventually to lay the foundations of a modern public health system.

MEDICAL ADVANCES

Hand in hand with sanitary reform went advances in medical science. There were more doctors and they were increasingly skilled, many of them aware of the close relationship between patients' health and their environment. Separate fever wards in hospitals helped cut down the spread of infection, and the growth of Foundling Hospitals contributed to a fall in the infant death rate. The establishment of dispensaries, offering free advice and medicine, was another important development contributing to improved health.

Anaesthetics, antiseptic surgery, together with Pasteur's work on microbes, still lay in the future; but by the mid-nineteenth century most of the machinery for creating better public health was in place. All that was needed was the will to use it.

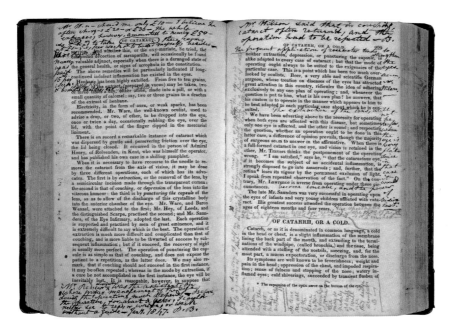

PATRICK BRONTË'S ANNOTATED VOLUME OF "MODERN DOMESTIC MEDICINE".

MEDICINE AND SANITATION

DOMESTIC LIFE

**THE APEX OF
SOCIETY: QUEEN
VICTORIA VISITS
ASTON HALL IN
WARWICKSHIRE.**

IN THE FIRST HALF of the nineteenth century – as at most other times in our history –
domestic life varied greatly according to the
social class of the family concerned.

The great country house, supporting a large family
and many guests, employed a huge range of servants:
grooms, gardeners, stable-lads, blacksmiths, dairy-
maids, footmen, cooks, house and scullery-maids and, at
the head of the hierarchy, the house-steward and the
housekeeper. The daily life of the family would involve a
good many outdoor occupations, like riding, shooting
and hunting, and the ladies would go out in their car-
riages, paying calls, perhaps, or simply to enjoy the
scenery, as Charlotte did with the Kay Shuttleworths
when she stayed in the Lake District. Indoors, music,
painting and letter-writing were the usual occupations

of the ladies, and in the evening men and women might
join in listening to and making music or playing cards
together before the gentlemen retired to their smoking
and billiards.

Among people of this class, eating was an important
social event, a fact reflected in the literature of the
period. Breakfast and luncheon were insubstantial
meals compared with the main one, dinner, which was
eaten around seven or eight o'clock in the evening. It
was not until the 1840s, when it became fashionable to
dine later, that afternoon tea became common. In the
early part of the century, callers would be offered cakes
and wine; tea gradually replaced this custom, although
not without some opposition!

MIDDLE-CLASS LIFE

Middle-class domestic life varied a good deal according
to how strongly the lady of the house aspired to be fashionable. In many farmhouses even substantial farmers
still expected to dine with their employees – as Hardy's
humbler Mr Crick does with his farm-hands in *Tess of
the d'Urbervilles* – and farm servants were expected to
"live-in" until they married, as Tess and Angel do. In
households of this kind, housewife and maids worked
side by side in the dairy or still-room, just as the master
and his men worked the fields together.

Where families aspired to a more genteel way of life,
the separation between mistress and servants was much
sharper: meals were taken separately and a much more
formal relationship was maintained between them.
Even so, long years of living with and working for the
same family inevitably led to an intimacy between many

employers and servants of the kind which bound the Brontës and their loyal servants, Tabby and Martha.

The women in these middle-class households led much the same kind of lives as their better-off counterparts. In addition to drawing and painting and perhaps making music, they would spend much of their time, as soon as they were old enough, sewing. Sewing-machines did not come into general use until the 1860s, and a dressmaker would be employed only to make more important clothes – fittings for these were very time-consuming – so women were much occupied providing underclothing and other everyday garments. A large wardrobe was necessary not only because people's social lives demanded a range of clothes suitable for different occasions, but also because wash-days were so infrequent, often as seldom as once a month.

Possessing an income sufficient to maintain a stable and support both carriage and riding-horses provided increased independence for middle-class women. The Bennet sisters in *Pride and Prejudice* are hampered, we remember, by not having ready access to their father's horses because they are needed on the farm. Not all young ladies were able or strong-minded enough to resist their mother's opposition to walking "in all this dirt" as Elizabeth does when she insists on going to see Jane at Netherfield. Readily available horses meant that women were free to make calls, go shopping, or simply escape briefly from the tedium of much of their daily lives.

WORKING PEOPLE

Lower down the social scale people's lives were affected mainly by the type of house or rooms in which the family lived. At the very bottom of this scale , it is no wonder that men, if they could afford it, often escaped the bleak and comfortless rooms of home to spend their leisure in the cheerful, brightly lit local public houses. Working people had their main meal in the middle of the day, with only a light snack in the morning and evening; but many living in cheap lodging houses had no cooking facilities at all and had to buy food from street-vendors,

cookhouses or the more up-market "chop houses", where men only could buy "meat and two veg", washed down by porter.

While the lot of the very poor was extremely grim, skilled working men and their families enjoyed a more comfortable life. The children might well go to school until the age of ten or twelve and they would be well, if plainly, fed. However, even among this class, large families led to dreadful overcrowding, and girls as young as ten were often sent away as live-in servants to ease the burden on their families.

THE ROYAL FAMILY

By the middle of the century, at the apex of society, Queen Victoria and Prince Albert were setting an example of domesticity which became a model, especially for the middle classes. Prince Albert not only planned and supervised all the details of his children's education, but he and the Queen took every opportunity to enjoy a relaxed family life, particularly when in the relative privacy of Osborne House and Balmoral. The children were encouraged to cultivate their own gardens and enjoyed long walks and picnics with their parents in a domestic life which was a far cry from the formality which had prevailed in the Royal Family during previous generations.

"AN ENGLISH WORKMAN AND HIS FAMILY", BY GEORGE CRUIKSHANK, FROM HIS FAMOUS MORAL NARRATIVE "THE BOTTLE", 1847.

DOMESTIC LIFE

LITERARY CONTEMPORARIES

WILLIAM MAKEPEACE THACKERAY (1811–1863). HE WAS, OF ALL CHARLOTTE'S CONTEMPORARIES, THE WRITER SHE MOST ADMIRED.

EMILY DICKINSON (1830–1886). THE TWO EMILYS WOULD HAVE UNDERSTOOD EACH OTHER.

THE BRONTËS' LIVES, short as they were, overlapped with many of the greatest names in English literature. When Anne, the youngest of the Brontë children, was born in 1820, Jane Austen had been dead for three years, but all the major Romantic poets were still alive: Wordsworth, Coleridge, Byron, Shelley, Keats. The grand old man of the Romantic movement, Wordsworth, was to outlive all the Brontë children except Charlotte. Walter Scott, such a formative influence on their writings, would live for another twelve years after Anne's birth. Imagine their grief when news reached them that "the great Sir Walter", as Charlotte called him, had died.

THE AMERICAN EMILY

In 1820, across the Atlantic, three of the greatest American writers were growing up: Nathaniel Hawthorne was sixteen, and Herman Melville and Walt Whitman were just one year old. Ten years later, when Emily Brontë was twelve, there was born in New England another poet with whom she might have found much in common; but Emily Dickinson's poetry was not published until after her death in 1886, nearly forty years after publication of *Wuthering Heights*. One wonders if she knew of that other Emily in Haworth; had she read her novel? Certainly, Emily Brontë would have understood and recognized qualities in Emily Dickinson which she

shared: the mystical identification with the natural world, a kind of directness and honesty and courage which marks them both, even the reluctance to move from the safe confines of home.

DICKENS AND THACKERAY

Back in 1820 and at home in England, Charles Dickens – the giant among Victorian novelists – was eight. One year older was Charlotte's literary hero, Thackeray, of whom she was to write later to Smith Williams, "it is him I at heart reverence with all my strength". Charlotte was to dedicate her second revised edition of *Jane Eyre* to Thackeray, and in her preface to that edition she justifies her dedication in the following terms:

ELIZABETH GASKELL AND HARRIET MARTINEAU

Is the satirist of 'Vanity Fair' admired in high places? I cannot tell … I think I see in him an intellect profounder and more unique than his contemporaries have yet recognised; because I regard him as the first social regenerator of the day, as the very master of the working corps who would restore to rectitude the warped system of things.

Writing to Smith Williams twelve days before the publication of *Jane Eyre*, Charlotte had voiced a sense of her own inadequacy in relation to

… the eminent writers you mention – Mr Thackeray, Mr Dickens … doubtless enjoyed facilities for observation such as I have not; certainly they possess a knowledge of the world, whether intuitive or acquired, such as I can lay no claim to – and this gives their writings an importance and a variety greatly beyond what I can offer the public.

Later in their correspondence, Smith Williams commented on similarities between *Jane Eyre* and *David Copperfield*, and Charlotte replied:

I have read 'David Copperfield'; it seems to me very good – admirable in some parts. You said it had affinity to 'Jane Eyre'. It has, now and then – only what an advantage has Dickens in his varied knowledge of men and things!

It was, perhaps, because of this sense of her own work reflecting much more limited experience than that of her greatest contemporaries that she later chose for *Shirley* both incidents and characters more rooted in the social and political issues of her time. In view of her own reservations, how astonished Charlotte would have been to read Lockhart's praises of *Jane Eyre*:

I have finished the adventures of Miss Jane Eyre, and think her far the cleverest that has written since Austen and Edgeworth were in their prime. Worth fifty Trollopes and Martineaus rolled into one counterpane, with fifty Dickenses and Bulwers to keep them company; but rather a brazen Miss …

Of her contemporary women novelists, Charlotte – at the end of her life – knew, of course, both Elizabeth Gaskell and Harriet Martineau. Harriet Martineau was well known in her lifetime as a passionate supporter of social reform, as the writer of the novel *Deerbrook* and, later, for her atheistical writings, which both shocked and dismayed Charlotte, as she explained:

It is the first exposition of avowed Atheism and Materialism I have ever seen … If this be Truth, Man or Woman who beholds her can but curse the day he or she was born.

Elizabeth Gaskell was an altogether safer and more comforting friend. Six years older than Charlotte, she published her first novel, *Mary Barton*, in 1848. It enjoyed both considerable criticism and wide popularity – depending on where the reader's sympathies lay – for its realistic portrayal of conditions in the industrial Manchester of the late 1830s and early 1840s. Dickens was so impressed by it that he recruited Mrs Gaskell to write for *Household Words*, his weekly periodical which was aimed at a more popular reader than *Blackwood's* or *The Edinburgh Review*. It was in *Household Words* that Elizabeth Gaskell's novels *Cranford* and *North and South* originally appeared in serial form.

Well known as a writer and a friend of Charlotte in her last years, Mrs Gaskell was a natural choice for Patrick to make when looking for "some established Author" to write his daughter's biography.

A SCENE FROM THACKERAY'S MASTERPIECE, "VANITY FAIR", WHICH SHOWS THE PROTAGONIST, BECKY SHARP, IN BRUSSELS.

THE LEGACY OF THE

5BRONTËS

IT IS DIFFICULT to imagine a world in which the Brontës never lived. *Jane Eyre* and *Wuthering Heights* are not only famous; they have so captured the imaginations of generations of readers that the characters and events of the novels live on in their minds and in the Brontë landscape.

It is the Brontës' ability to involve the reader in their imaginative worlds that brings people flocking to Haworth; the small Yorkshire town vies with Stratford-upon-Avon as a literary shrine. People come, of course, from all over the world and are to be seen not only in the Museum but – in all weathers – making the long pilgrimage climb to Top Withens to see for themselves Cathy's moorland heaven.

People have read *Jane Eyre* and *Wuthering Heights* in one of more than twenty different languages; they bring to their understanding of them myriad cultural backgrounds, some so different that one wonders what attraction the Brontës have for them. A Japanese visitor on the moors explained that, for him and his countrymen and women, it was, in his opinion, the common language of tragedy which they all spoke.

His perception of the Brontës' appeal to the public would explain why many are drawn to Haworth and the moors not only because of the novels and poems but because of their lives. Theirs is a moving story, and people have responded to it emotionally and personally. Without the books they wrote, however, we would know nothing of this Yorkshire family living obscure lives in the first half of the nineteenth century; they would have joined the many others, now forgotten, in the Haworth graveyard.

It is for their literary works that we remember them; their books are their immortality here. Students at schools and universities across the world read, are examined and write learned theses on them. Biographers examine their lives, literary critics their writing. They bring to their interpretations and appreciation their own perspectives, be they feminist, Marxist or whatever.

By the centenary of Charlotte's birth in 1916, Herbert Wroot could write of the novels: "dramatized versions have been printed in the United States, France, Germany, Italy, and Denmark". Plays of the novels continue to be produced on the stage, the most recent a successful adaptation of *Villette* by Judith Adams. They have been read on radio and dramatized for both television and cinema, reaching a wider and more popular audience than the Brontës could have imagined.

Nor would they have dreamt that, in December 1893, three days before the forty-fifth anniversary of Emily's death, there would be a meeting in Bradford Town Hall "to consider the advisability of forming a Brontë Society and Museum". Such was the enthusiasm and response for the proposal that they resolved "That a Brontë Society be and is hereby formed" and that one of its objectives should be to "establish a museum".

The Museum today continues to fulfil these objectives. Unlike many literary societies, the Brontë Society has continued to flourish, as its many branches across the world – from Haworth to Australia, from Ireland to Japan – bear witness.

SAMANTHA MORTON AS THE EPONYMOUS HEROINE IN THE 1997 FILM VERSION OF "JANE EYRE".

BIOGRAPHIES

SINCE MRS GASKELL'S *Life of Charlotte Brontë*, which was published in 1857, there have been a great many biographies of the Brontës, treating them either as individuals or as a family. Few literary figures have inspired such interest in their lives as well as their works.

In many ways it has been the misfortune of the Brontës to have been isolated, romantic figures whose tragic, early deaths aroused sympathy and pity in us all; such a reputation and response in their readers have meant that too often serious literary biography has been sacrificed to sensational and romanticized, melodramatic interpretation of both their lives and their works. Mrs Gaskell, of course, in her determination to protect and present Charlotte in the most sympathetic light, did not help; but her *Life* will always remain vitally impor-

THE HOUSE AT THORNTON WHERE THE YOUNGEST FOUR OF THE BRONTË CHILDREN WERE BORN.

tant to an understanding of them, written, as it was, so close in time to when the Brontës lived and with access to people who knew them.

MRS GASKELL

Leaving aside its biased slant and omission of important facts, Mrs Gaskell's *Life* is a delight to read. With the gift of the accomplished novelist that she was, she presents Charlotte and her world to us with a vividness, a sense of historical and social context which both inform and absorb the reader. Take, for instance, her description of Keighley, the nearest reasonably-sized town to Haworth:

Keighley is in process of transformation from a populous, old-fashioned village, into a still more populous and flourishing town. It is evident to the stranger that, as the gable-ended houses ... fall vacant, they are pulled down to allow of greater space for traffic and a more modern style of architecture. The quaint and narrow shop-windows of fifty years ago are giving way to large panes and plate-glass. Nearly every dwelling seems devoted to some branch of commerce ...

The town of Keighley never quite melts into country on the road to Haworth, although the houses become more sparse as the traveller journeys upwards to the grey round hills ...

Her strength here is in enabling us to see and experience the world which Charlotte and her siblings themselves saw and experienced. It was her declared intention to do just that. She begins Chapter II of the *Life* with:

THE "GUN GROUP"
PORTRAIT OF
CHARLOTTE,
EMILY, ANNE AND
BRANWELL, BY
BRANWELL.

For a right understanding of the life of my dear friend, Charlotte Brontë, it appears to me more necessary in her case than in most others, that the reader should be made acquainted with the peculiar forms of population and society amidst which her earliest years were passed …

While Mrs Gaskell is an invaluable source of information and detail, we need to remember that she was a novelist, not an historian. Her gifts include imaginative interpretation; and it is inevitable that both the facts behind it and the interpretation itself are open to challenge.

JULIET BARKER

The last forty years or so have seen the publication of the Winifred Gérin biographies of each of the Brontës, followed by others too numerous to mention here. By far the most important contribution to Brontë biography, however, since Mrs Gaskell's *Life* is Juliet Barker's *The Brontës*, a thousand-page volume published in 1994.

Juliet Barker has brought to her biography a wealth of detail, meticulously researched and absorbed into a coherent interpretation of the Brontës' lives. In particular, she helps to redress the imbalance of Mrs Gaskell's presenta-

tion of both Patrick and Branwell. Patrick's life is examined in close detail, from his early days in Ireland, his education at Cambridge, his courting of Maria, to his role as father and perpetual curate of Haworth. Like Mrs Gaskell, but with more objectivity than she showed, Juliet Barker places the Brontës firmly in their time; much of the biography is, of course, social history. If she sometimes treats Charlotte harshly, it is usually because she has sound source material on which to base her judgement.

Very readable, impressively indexed and annotated, the biography is essential reading for those seriously interested in the Brontës. It has been an invaluable, up-to-date source of information, clarification and verification for the writer of this book.

ADAPTATIONS
OF THE NOVELS

LAURENCE OLIVIER AND MERLE OBERON IN THE MGM CLASSIC FILM ADAPTATION OF "WUTHERING HEIGHTS".

TARA FITZGERALD AND TOBY STEPHENS IN "THE TENANT OF WILDFELL HALL".

THE LEGACY OF THE BRONTËS

A S *Jane Eyre* and *Wuthering Heights* have always been the most popular of the Brontë novels among readers, it is these two that have attracted the most interest from film-makers: both books have been dramatized on several occasions, with varying degrees of success.

Jane Eyre has been produced for the cinema no fewer than six times: the first version, a silent film, was produced in 1921, with a sound version following in 1934; further cinema adaptations were produced in 1944, 1957, 1971 and 1996. There have also been two television adaptations of the novel – a six-part series in 1983 and a feature-length film in 1997. *Wuthering Heights*, with its difficult structure and dark themes, is perhaps a more difficult novel to

adapt, but it has been filmed no less than three times: in 1939, 1970 and 1992. Some of the adaptations of these two novels are more memorable than others, while many are just plainly miscast. However, two of the best adaptations came from Hollywood's "golden age", both films have stood the test of time and are deserved "classics".

Wuthering Heights (1939) saw Laurence Olivier make his Hollywood debut as Heathcliff, opposite Merle Oberon as Cathy. The film used some of the major cinematic talents of its day: and won many prestigious awards. With a script by the novelist Aldous Huxley, the film dedicates itself to the first half of the book, ending with Cathy's death and, while this is not ideal, it is still a moving and gripping interpretation of Emily's only novel.

Aldous Huxley also contributed to the script of *Jane Eyre* (1943), a film notable, among other things, for a performance by a very young Elizabeth Taylor as Helen Burns. Orson Welles was a suitably intriguing Rochester, but Joan Fontaine's Jane was more prim than passionate and pretty rather than plain, a problem in other adaptations of the book. A few years later, the same actress was cast as Maxim de Winter's bewildered wife in *Rebecca*, a film based on Daphne du Maurier's gripping novel, which many view as a tribute to *Jane Eyre*.

Susannah York and George C. Scott had a stab at Jane and Rochester in 1971, in a relatively dull version of the book, again with an actress too sweet and coy to convey a realistic Jane. The same era also produced an uninspiring *Wuthering Heights*, with future James Bond Timothy Dalton as Heathcliff and Anna Calder Marshall as Cathy. Dalton has the distinction of being the only actor to play both Heathcliff and Rochester: he was cast as the latter in the 1983 television series of *Jane Eyre*.

More recent renditions of these two novels, though certainly not without their problems, have been somewhat more faithful to the authors' intentions. A 1992 version of *Wuthering Heights* paired Juliette Binoche and Ralph Fiennes as Heathcliff and Cathy/Catherine. The film was a brave attempt to film the whole novel in under two hours, and made fine use of the Yorkshire Moors as a backdrop. Interestingly, it draws Emily into her own novel, with Sinead O'Connor playing the writer as narrator of the film.

1996 saw Franco Zeffirelli's gloomy version of *Jane Eyre*. Although it condenses Jane's childhood experiences drastically, the two actresses who play Jane capture the nature of her character well – Anna Paquin is a particularly spirited and passionate young Jane, while in the actress playing the older Jane in this version, Charlotte Gainsbourg, we finally see a convincing adult heroine, "poor, obscure, plain, and little". Samantha Morton, who played Jane in the 1997 television film, is also cast well and proves moving and convincing as Jane alongside a capricious Ciaran Hinds as Rochester.

Anne's novels have not excited nearly as much attention from film makers. However, in 1996, the BBC/PBS produced an absorbing television series of *The Tenant of Wildfell Hall*, proving that Anne's work is certainly as suitable for the screen as her sisters'. The series was excellently cast, Tara Fitzgerald portrayed the self-sacrificing and morally upright Helen Graham/Huntingdon with reserve and dignity. Rupert Graves played Helen's husband as suitably lascivious and brutal, without lapsing into parody, and Toby Stephens was affecting as Helen's suitor Gilbert Markham. *The Tenant of Wildfell Hall* was a successful addition to Brontë adaptations: perhaps we can now look forward to *Agnes Grey* on screen.

It is not just the cinema and television that have produced adaptations of the novels. By 1816, the centenary of Charlotte's birth, there were dramatic versions of *Jane Eyre* in the United States, France, Germany, Italy and Denmark. Since then, of course, there have been many radio and stage productions of the Brontë novels, the most surprising of which is the spectacular musical of *Wuthering Heights*, starring Cliff Richard as Heathcliff.

No discussion of the dramatizations of the novels would be complete without Charlotte's own comments to Smith Williams when she heard that *Jane Eyre, The Secrets of Thornfield Manor* had found its way on to the London Stage in February 1848:

A representation of 'Jane Eyre' at a minor theatre would no doubt be a rather afflicting spectacle to the author of that work. I suppose all would be woefully exaggerated and painfully vulgarized by the actors and actresses on the stage. What, I cannot help asking myself, would they make of Mr Rochester? And the picture my fancy conjures up by way of reply is a somewhat humiliating one. What would they make of Jane Eyre? I see something very pert and very affected as an answer to that query.

SAMANTHA MORTON AND CIARAN HINDS AS JANE AND ROCHESTER

THE MUSEUM

THE BRONTË SOCIETY, one of the world's most famous literary societies, was formed in 1893. One of its major objectives was to

establish a Museum to contain not only drawings, manuscripts, paintings, and other personal relics of the Brontë family, but all editions of their works, the writing of authors upon these works, or upon any member of the family, together with photographs of places or premises with which the family was associated.

It was not until 1928 that the Parsonage was bought — at the cost of £3000 — from the Church Trustees by Sir

James Roberts and given to the Brontë Society as a permanent home for its museum.

BRONTËANA

By that time, of course, most of the Brontë possessions were scattered to the four winds, and it has been the painstaking task of the Society to return as many of them as possible to the Parsonage. That task continues today, with purchases being made at auctions throughout the world; down the years there have been generous gifts from owners of Brontëana, and the Museum now has a wealth of manuscripts, paintings and drawings, fur-

ON LOAN TO THE MUSEUM IS THE TABLE ON WHICH THE BRONTË SISTERS WROTE THEIR NOVELS. IT IS EASILY RECOGNIZABLE FROM EMILY'S SKETCH IN THE 1837 DIARY PAPER.

niture and other artefacts associated with the family.

So far as possible, and where contemporary records exist, the house has been restored and furnished to look as it would have done in the Brontës' time. All the furniture now in the Museum belonged to the Brontës, but much of it dates from the 1850s when Charlotte had become famous and was in a position to re-furnish the Parsonage. Some of the rooms, like the dining room, the study and Patrick's bedroom, are arranged to look as if they are being lived in; others, like Charlotte's bedroom, are set out as showcases, with the family's possessions on display. Of all the rooms in the Museum, the one which most differs from the original is the kitchen. Though reconstructed to look as much like the Brontë kitchen as possible, it is smaller than the one they knew, the back kitchen having been pulled down by Patrick Brontë's successor, Mr Wade. He also built a new gable wing to the side of the Parsonage which transformed the kitchen into an interior room, since it blocked its only window.

The new wing now houses the Exhibition Room upstairs and the library and Bonnell Room downstairs. Visitors to the Museum progress automatically from the original building into the Exhibition Room, which outlines the lives of the Brontë family and explains and displays their literary and artistic works. Temporary exhibitions on specific Brontë subjects are also displayed here, as is the Apostles' Cupboard, so vividly described in *Jane Eyre*.

Below the Exhibition Room are the library and the Bonnell Room, named after an American who left a substantial part of his rare collection of Brontë manuscripts to the Museum in the late 1920s. The room serves as a second exhibition area, where Brontë manuscripts and drawings are displayed according to themes – a recent exhibition here, for instance, has been of letters written to or by the Brontës.

In front of the Bonnell Room and beside the kitchen is the Library, a room not open to Museum visitors, but available – by appointment – to anyone wishing to research into the Brontë archives. The librarians are on hand to offer help and specialist information and knowledge to those interested in or writing about the Brontës.

Down a curved, stone staircase at the back of the entrance hall is another room not open to the ordinary Museum visitor. It is the small vaulted cellar which, no doubt, fed the young Brontës' imaginations with pictures of castle dungeons. It is now used as a small lecture room and sometimes as a gathering place for school parties. The educational programme has flourished in recent years – the Museum has received a prestigious award for its work in this field – and students of all ages and from all parts of the world come to see where the Brontës lived and to learn about their works.

Because of pressure on space at the Parsonage itself, the Society recently purchased a house in Main Street, where much of the administration is carried out, and where school groups, teachers and other interested adults can take part in educational and creative workshops.

A popular place with visitors is the Museum shop at the rear of the Parsonage. It sells cards, posters and new books associated with the Brontës, and it also carries a good selection of second-hand, often out-of-print Brontë books and some specially commissioned gifts, like replicas of the sisters' writing desks or Emily's christening mug.

SOME PLACES IN THE NOVELS

NORTON CONYERS: IT HAS BEEN THOUGHT THAT THE HOUSE WAS A MODEL FOR THORNFIELD IN "JANE EYRE", BUT IT IS BY NO MEANS CERTAIN THAT CHARLOTTE EVER WENT THERE.

WE HAVE ALREADY SEEN how a number of places the Brontës knew found their way into the novels: Cowan Bridge and The Rydings in *Jane Eyre*, the moors in *Wuthering Heights*; Brussels and the Pensionnat Heger in *The Professor* and *Villette*, Oakwell Hall and the Red House in *Shirley*.

There are others, however, which deserve mention here. Writers of fiction, of course, call on all their experience, both actual and imaginary, to create their works, and it would be surprising if some of the places in the novels were not inspired by several different locations.

JANE EYRE

Thornfield Hall in *Jane Eyre* is probably just such a house. The external description of Thornfield Hall fits that of Ellen Nussey's house, The Rydings; but there are other contenders for its inspiration. Norton Conyers, a large Jacobean house north of Ripon, has traditionally been one of them, although it is by no means certain that Charlotte ever saw the house. If she did, it would have been on a visit to the Graham family there when she went with her employers, the Sidgwicks, to stay at "Swarcliffe" near Harrogate. Certainly, the interior of Norton Conyers, with its dark oak panelling and impressive staircase, bears a close resemblance to that of Thornfield, even to the extent of having a room in the attic where, legend has it, a mad woman was kept. No doubt many other big houses shared these features with Thornfield.

Another more likely inspiration for Thornfield is North Lees, a castellated manor house a few miles from Hathersage in Derbyshire, which becomes the village Morton in *Jane Eyre*. That Charlotte knew the area is indisputable: she stayed at the vicarage there with Ellen Nussey, whose brother Henry was vicar of Hathersage from 1845 to 1847.

There are a number of indications that she used names and places associated with the town as material for *Jane Eyre*, including the surname of her heroine. In Hathersage Church are to be found brasses of the Eyre family, memorials to the owners of North Lees dating back to the fifteenth century. The Apostles' Cupboard, which Charlotte describes in such detail in *Jane Eyre*, is now in the Brontë Parsonage Museum, but until 1862 it was at North Lees. A further link between North Lees and Thornfield is to be found in their names: "North" becomes "thorn" backwards and "lee" or "lea" means "field".

There are other connections, too: the only rich man in St John Rivers' parish is "Mr Oliver, the proprietor of a needle-factory" – the mills in Hathersage, unlike those in Haworth, produced needles, not textiles. St John and his sisters live at Moor House, almost certainly the actual house Moorseats.

Wycoller Hall in Lancashire has been associated with the last house described in *Jane Eyre*, Ferndean Manor. It is here that Jane finally finds the blinded and dispirited Rochester after the death of Bertha in the fire at Thornfield. Wycoller is a lovely remote hamlet, now the centre of a Country Park. Its stone houses nestle in a deep valley through which a shallow stream meanders under old gritstone bridges. The Hall, a ruin, belonged to the Cunliffe family, one of whom – Elizabeth – became an Eyre on her second marriage. Even in Charlotte's day the Hall had very probably fallen into disrepair and disuse; its owner died heavily in debt.

WUTHERING HEIGHTS

The specific places named in *Wuthering Heights* are perhaps more difficult to identify, even tentatively. The *site* of the Heights is fairly generally accepted as being that of Top Withens, but the house itself is clearly not the rather modest farmhouse whose ruins we see there today. Probable inspirations for the house of Wuthering Heights are High Sunderland Hall and Shibden Hall near Halifax; Emily would have known them both well – at least externally – during her time at Law Hill. Certainly the nude cherubs on either side of the front door at High Sunderland Hall – long since demolished – might well have been her models for the "shameless little boys" she describes at the Heights. Emily would also, incidentally, have heard the history of the Walker family of Walterclough Hall – just a mile from Law Hill – who, in the eighteenth century, had been financially ruined as a result of taking into their home an orphan boy, Jack Sharp.

Thrushcross Grange is even more difficult to identify. Although it has often been linked to Ponden Hall, and the site may be right, the house in the novel is a much grander one than Ponden. It is very probable that Emily, when creating the houses – rather than the landscape – relied more on her imagination, and perhaps on her reading, than on actuality.

THE APOSTLES' CUPBOARD, SO VIVIDLY DESCRIBED IN "JANE EYRE".

TOP WITHENS, ALMOST CERTAINLY THE SITE OF WUTHERING HEIGHTS.

INDEX

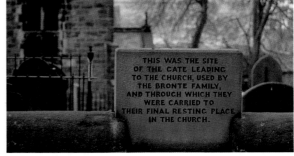

THIS WAS THE SITE OF THE GATE LEADING TO THE CHURCH, USED BY THE BRONTE FAMILY, AND THROUGH WHICH THEY WERE TO THEIR FINAL RESTING PLACE IN THE CHURCH.

BIBLIOGRAPHY

Alexander, C. & Sellars, J. *The Art of The Brontës* (Cambridge University Press, 1995)

Allott, M. ed. by *Charlotte Brontë Jane Eyre and Villette, A Casebook* (Macmillan Education, 1973)

Allott, M. ed. by *Emily Brontë, Wuthering Heights, A Casebook* (Macmillan and Co Ltd., 1979)

Armytage, W.H.G. *Four Hundred Years of English Education* (Cambridge University Press, 1964)

Babbage, B.H. *Report to the General Board of Health, on a Preliminary Inquiry into the Sewerage, Drainage, and Supply of Water, and the Sanitary Condition of the Inhabitants of the Hamlet of Haworth* (HMSO, 1850)

Barker, Juliet *The Brontës* (Weidenfeld and Nicolson, 1994)

Brontë, Anne *Agnes Grey*, ed. A. Goreau (Penguin, 1988)

Brontë, Anne *The Tenant of Wildfell Hall*, ed. G.D. Hargreaves (Penguin, 1985)

Brontë, Charlotte *Jane Eyre*, ed. Margaret Smith (Oxford University Press, 1981)

Brontë, Charlotte *Shirley*, ed. H. Rosengarten and Margaret Smith (Oxford University Press, 1981)

Brontë, Charlotte *The Professor* (Oxford University Press, 1906)

Brontë, Charlotte *Villette* (Penguin Books, 1979)

Brontë, Emily *The Complete Poems of Emily Jane Brontë*, ed. C.W. Hatfield (Columbia University Press, 1941)

Brontë, Emily *Wuthering Heights*, ed. W. Sale (W.W. Norton & Company, 1972)

Brontës, The *Selected Poems*, ed. Juliet Barker (J.M. Dent & Sons Ltd. & Charles E. Tuttle Co. Inc., 1985)

Cowrie, Donald *Belgium, The Land and the People* (A.S. Barnes & Co. Inc., 1977)

Cruise O'Brien, M. & C. *Ireland, A Concise History* (Thames & Hudson, 1985)

Cusack, C.F. *The Illustrated History of Ireland* (The Mansfield Publishing Co., 1986)

Davies, Hunter *A Walk Around the Lakes* (Weidenfeld & Nicolson, 1979)

Foster, R.F. *The Oxford Illustrated History of Ireland* (Oxford University Press, 1991)

Frank, Katherine *Emily Brontë, A Chainless Soul* (Hamish Hamilton, 1990)

Fraser, Rebecca *Charlotte Brontë* (Methuen London, 1988)

Freethy, R. & M. *Discovering Coastal Yorkshire* (John Donald Publishers Ltd., 1992)

Gaskell, Elizabeth *The Life of Charlotte Brontë* (Smith, Elder & Co., 1873)

Gérin, Winifred *Anne Brontë* (Allen Lane, 1959)

Gérin, Winifred *Charlotte Brontë, The Evolution of Genius* (Oxford University Press, 1967)

Gérin, Winifred *Emily Brontë, A Biography* (Oxford University Press, 1971)

Gerrard, C. *Gothic* (The English Review, Vol. 1, Issue 3, February 1991)

Gray, Peter *The Irish Famine* (Thames & Hudson, 1995)

Gregg, Pauline *A Social and Economic History of Britain, 1760–1980* (Harrap, 1950)

Hewish, John *Emily Brontë, A Critical and Biographical Study* (Macmillan, 1969)

Hibbert, C. *London, The Biography of a City* (Longmans, 1969)

Kee, Robert *Ireland, A History* (Weidenfeld and Nicolson, 1980)

Kitson Clark, G. *The Making of Victorian England* (Methuen, 1962)

Lloyd Evans, B. and G. *Everyman's Companion to the Brontës* (J.M. Dent & Sons Ltd., 1982)

Longford, E. *Victoria R.I* (Weidenfeld and Nicolson, 1964)

Lyon, Margot *Belgium* (Thames and Hudson, 1971)

MacDonagh, O. *Early Victorian Government 1830–1870* (Weidenfeld and Nicolson, 1977)

Marshall, Dorothy *The Life and Times of Victoria* (Weidenfeld and Nicolson, 1972)

Mayhew, Henry *London Labour and the London Poor*, ed. V. Neuburg (Penguin Books, 1985)

Omond, G. *Belgium* (A. & C. Black, 1908)

Pool, P.A. *The History of the Town and Borough of Penzance* (The Corporation of Penzance, 1974)

Pool, P.A.S. *The Branwell Connection* (Brontë Society Transactions, Vol. 18, 1983)

Postgate, R. *Story of a Year, 1848* (Jonathan Cape, 1955)

Ratchford, F. *The Brontës Web of Childhood* (Columbia University Press, 1941)

Rees, Edgar *Old Penzance* (pub. by the Author, 1956)

Rowntree, Arthur ed. by *The History of Scarborough* (J.M. Dent & Sons Ltd., 1931)

Shepherd, F. *The History of London 1808–1870: The Infernal Wen* (Secker and Warburg, 1971)

Smith, Margaret ed. by *The Letters of Charlotte Brontë* (Oxford University Press, 1995)

Spark, Muriel, selected by *The Brontë Letters* (Macmillan, 1966)

Trevelyan, G.M. *English Social History* (Longmans, Green and Co., 1942)

Trevelyan, G.M. *History of England* (Longmans, Green and Co., 1952)

White, L.W. & Shanahan, E.W. *The Industrial Revolution and the Economic World of To-Day* (Longmans, Green and Co., 1932)

Wickwar, W.H. *The Struggle for the Freedom of the Press, 1819–1832* (Allen and Unwin, 1928)

Wilde, Lady *Ancient Cures, Charms, and Usages of Ireland* (Ward & Downey, 1890)

Wilks, Brian *The Brontës*, (Hamlyn, 1975)

Wise, T.J. and Symington, J.A. ed. by *The Brontës: Their Lives, Friendships and Correspondence – 4 Vols.* (Oxford, Basil Blackwell, 1932)

Woodham-Smith, Cecil *The Great Hunger, Ireland 1845–9* (Hamish Hamilton, 1962)

Woodward, L. *The Age of Reform 1815–1870* (Oxford University Press, 1962)

Young, G.M. *Early Victorian England 1830–1865* (Oxford University Press, 1934)

THE WORLD OF THE BRONTËS

ACKNOWLEDGMENTS

ANNE BRONTË,
"WOMAN GAZING
AT A SUNRISE
OVER A SEASCAPE",
NOVEMBER 13, 1839.

AUTHOR'S NOTE:

I should like to express my gratitude to the following for permission to quote from their books: Juliet Barker (*The Brontës*), and Margaret Smith (*The Letters of Charlotte Brontë*, published in 1995 – letters from this edition are quoted by permission of the Oxford University Press). I am also most grateful to Blackwell Publishers Ltd. for their permission to quote from letters included in: *The Brontës – Their Lives, Friendships & Correspondence* (4 vols.) by Wise and Symington. I should like to express my thanks for the help I have received at the following: The Brontë Parsonage Museum Library, Cambridge Central Library, Girton College Library, Long Road Sixth Form College Library, Penzance Library.

I should also like to thank all those who have supported me in various ways in the writing of this book, particularly Robert Barnard, John and Margaret Bowker, Amanda Ferri, Lucy Munby and Jane Sellars. I owe a special debt of gratitude to Anne Dinsdale, librarian at the Brontë Parsonage Museum: her advice and help with providing material and reading this text have been invaluable and always so patiently and courteously given.

THE BRONTË SOCIETY

The Brontë Society was founded in 1893 to encourage interest in the lives and works of the Brontë family. In 1928, it acquired, by gift, the Parsonage at Haworth, which has ever since been a museum to the family. The Brontë Society publishes an academic journal, *Transactions*, has an extensive library, sponsors lectures and runs excursions and educational programmes. Anyone interested in belonging to the Society should write to:

The Membership Secretary,
The Brontë Parsonage Museum,
Haworth,
Keighley,
West Yorkshire
BD22 8DR

THE BRONTË PARSONAGE MUSEUM

Opening Times:
1.00am–5.00pm (April–September)
11.00am–4.30pm (October–March)
Closed 13th January–7th February,
24th–27th December
Telephone: 01535 642323
Fax: 01535 647131

The publishers would like to thank the following sources for their kind permission to reproduce the pictures in this book:

Lorna Ainger 72t. ©BBC Picture Library 62–3, 125t, 134c. The Bridgeman Art Library, London/*Bradford 1825–33*, John Wilson Anderson, Bradford Art Galleries and Museums 121; *Dark Landscape in the Black Country*, Constantin Emile Meunier (1831–1905) Giraudon/Musee D'Orsay 104; *General Post Office, St. Martin le Grand, 1852.* Lithograph by T.Picken after drawing by W.Simpson, Guildhall Library, Corporation of London 103; *Eton College from the Terrace of Windsor Castle*, Richard Bankes Harraden 1778–1862, Leger Gallery, London 117t; *The Dinner Hour, Wigan*, Eyre Crowe, 1874, Manchester City Art Galleries 120; *Lady in Grey*, Daniel MacNee, 1859, National Gallery Scotland 36; *The Slavedeck of the Albaroz, Prize to the H.M.S. Albatros*, Daniel Henry Meynell 1865, National Maritime Museum, London 118; *Rochester and Jane Eyre*, Frederick Walker (1840–75), Private Collection 69; *Victoria: Visit to Warwickshire, Aston Hall* after R.P. Leitch, Private Collection 128; *The Governess*, Richard Redgrave, 1844, V&A 58. ©The Bronte Society 1, 2, 3, 5, 12–15, 18–23, 25, 26, 28, 29, 31–35, 38, 39, 40, 41b, 42, 44, 46, 47, 50, 51, 54, 55, 59, 64, 65, 67, 70, 71, 73, 74, 76–81, 85, 90, 101, 102, 110, 115c, 117b, 126b, 127, 136–9, 141t, 144, endpapers. Corbis UK/Bettmann 130bl; Bob Krist 87. Mary Evans Picture Library 52, 53, 66, 98, 100, 106, 111-113, 115tr, 119, 124, 125b, 126, 129, 130tr, 131. Ronald Grant Archive/ 1943 Two Cities Films 57; 1939 Samuel Goldwyn 60, 68, 75, 134t. Image Select 41t/Ann Ronan 107, 109, 114, 122, 123. Images Colour Library 84. Kobal Collection/1996 Rochester/Miramax 37, 72b; United Artists 48. Sarah Larter 116, 142. London Weekend Television Copyright/Conway Van Gelder Ltd. 132, Larry Dalzell Associates Ltd., Conway Van Gelder Ltd., Stagecoach Management 135. National Portrait Gallery, London 10, 24, 45. M. Pechere 43. Rex Features Ltd./Clive Coote, Paramount, 1992 61b/Mega Productions Inc. 57t/Sipa 56, 61t. ©Simon Warner 4, 7, 16, 18–9, 27, 30, 82, 86, 91–97, 99, 108, 140, 141b. West Yorkshire Archive Service, Bradford (ref: 81D85/7/1) 17.

Every effort has been made to acknowledge correctly and contact the source and/or copyright holder of each picture, and Carlton Books Limited apologizes for any unintentional errors or omissions which will be corrected in future editions of this book.